How to Double Your Child's Grades in School

REVISED EDITION

How to Double Your Child's Grades in School

Build brilliance and leadership into your child—from kindergarten to college—in just 5 minutes a day

EUGENE M. SCHWARTZ

BARNES & NOBLE BOOKS

NEW YORK

Thanks to Dr. Joyce McPeake Robinson for her help

1999 Barnes & Noble Books

ISBN: 0-7607-1193-3

Text design and electronic pagination by Carole Desnoes

Printed and bound in the United States of America

99 00 01 02 M 9 8 7 6 5 4 3 2 1

RRD-H

CONTENTS

PREFACE

In 1964, Eugene Schwartz published the first edition of *How to Double Your Child's Grades in School.* He was overwhelmed by the number of parents and top educators around the world who wrote and told him how successful his simple program was. He also witnessed the results firsthand by using the system with his own son Michael.

In 1994, it became Gene's dream to completely revise and update the book so his own grandson could benefit from it. Unfortunately, Gene passed away in September 1995 while he was updating the book. His wife, Barbara, in conjunction with Dr. Joyce McPeake Robinson, has fulfilled his mission by completing the revision of the book to enable new generations of students to benefit from his timeless wisdom and insight. Dr. Robinson (Head of School, The Dwight School, Manhattan, New York City) has updated the book's examples and has integrated ideas from current top educational theory. Dr. Robinson's credentials include a bachelor's degree in English from Tufts University and a master's degree in English and a doctorate in reading and English language from Boston University.

The best introduction to this latest edition is still the preface from Mr. Schwartz's own first revised edition published in 1976:

> I had no idea when I wrote this book ten years ago that over 250,000 people would use it to improve their children's power to learn, and indeed, to improve their own power to learn. I had no idea that it would be adopted by hundreds of teachers, dozens of high schools, and even a major university as a supplementary text. Nor that it would be translated into

several languages and sell tens of thousands of additional copies in Europe.

All this was a surprise—a monumental surprise. For all I was trying to do, when I wrote it, was teach one parent—you—how to help one child—your child—get out of school what he or she should get out of it.

The worst thing in life is to have talent and not be able to use it. To have brains and not be able to harness them. To have potential that never becomes more than potential because someone doesn't show you how to actualize it.

Kids are so smart they frighten you—if you give them a chance to show their smartness. Since this book was written, I have personally taught, and supervised the teaching of, a sufficient number of "slow learners." In the most dramatic case, these were children from the absolute bottom of the first and second grades in a Harlem public school. One of them was labeled "brain-damaged." In three months, he became the assistant teacher of the class, and that crippling label was removed forever. The others simply became "smart," because someone finally made learning make sense for them. And once you show a child—any child—how to make learning make sense, that child will just "gobble up" the world of ideas.

I have never met a stupid child. I have met many, many children who were labeled "stupid" and who then went on to thrill me by creating their own sonnets, or philosophies, once they had really been shown how.

INTRODUCTION

• • •

A Short Survival Course for
Children in Tomorrow's World

What Top Grades Really Mean
to Your Child's Future

Let me be frank right at the start. In this modern, scientific world of ours, success or failure is molded in the classrooms of your school.

This all-important fact must be repeated over and over again: *No matter what the gender of your children—boy or girl—the quality of their future lives will be determined by their performance in school.*

By this I mean that their future income, the station they attain in life, even the satisfaction they get out of their sparetime activities—will be decided by their ability to keep up with their classmates in school, or forge ahead of them.

Does this sound impossible? Then consider these cold, hard facts:

- About ONE-THIRD of your child's life will be spent in school: 10,000 hours in elementary school, 6,000 hours in high school, and 6,000 hours or more in college. **A Third of Your Child's Life Will Be Spent in School**

1

- Almost everything that happens to those children in school will depend on their ability not only to master facts and think critically. They also need to know how to master material. On the basis of your child's performance in class, your boy or girl will be branded as slow or fast, or as a leader or a follower.

  Your Child's Performance in School Is Crucial

- Progress through school, the amount of real education, will depend entirely on grades. These grades will determine whether a student will be placed in a slow or fast group, with the best teachers or the worst, allowed to take advanced subjects and foreign languages in a college-preparatory class, or be barred from advancement.

  Real Education Will Depend Entirely on Grades

- A college education is the great open door to the top futures of tomorrow. Advances in science and technology also require advanced knowledge and skills to earn high salaries. With college, your son or daughter can earn millions more in a lifetime.

  Getting Ahead in College Is Worth Millions

- Even higher grades are required for your children to earn scholarships, scholarships that can save you thousands of dollars on their college costs, get them into the institutions of their choice rather than a second-best compromise, and perhaps even mean the difference between going or not going to college at all.

  Higher Grades Now Can Save Thousands

This then is the effect learning will have on your children by the time they are eighteen years old—ready to enter college.

These grades will determine their self-image and self-confidence, rate them with teachers and their fellow students, open up or block access to dozens of special advantages, and finally admit them to the brilliant world of top colleges.

But this entree to college—this real step upward—is only the beginning, for it is in college and beyond that the competition really stiffens. And the ability to master facts—to really understand what your child is doing—pays off far beyond your fondest dreams.

Consider These Further Facts

- Once in college, grades often determine the kind of job your child is offered when he or she gets out. Even today, the country's largest corporations, top employers, and graduate schools set their sights on the top 10 percent of the class. Usually they will not even consider anyone outside that select group.

  Top Employers and Graduate Schools Demand Top Grades

- From the moment your child graduates, the same sink-or-swim story repeats itself, time and time again. At every turning point in his or her career, your child will reap benefits from the priceless ability to absorb, master, and use information. Research about how the brain learns shows that young people can alter their mind patterns, making them better learners. With the right learning situations, they will have the opportunity to change their lives forever.

  Your Child Will Reap Lifelong Benefits

Here Are a Few of These Payoff Situations

- Your child can expect to take dozens of crucial tests throughout youth and adult life: A licensing test for a profession or vocation. A graduate study test for an advanced degree. A qualification test that

  Tests Will Always Demand the Ability to Absorb, Master, and Use Information

could get him or her an appointment to Annapolis, or a big promotion in a corporation. Or simply any of the tests that enable your child to drive a car, own a boat, repair a computer.

- Plus, of course, the job advancement tests given as often as once a year, every year, for the rest of his or her life. Tests determine your child's rate of progress, yearly pay scale, selection for special managerial staffs, or expensive training to prepare for a better position. They can decide if your child will break ahead of the field and go forward as fast as he or she can— even whether your child will be forced to retire too early, take a less demanding job, or continue at the top as before.

Tests Determine Your Child's Rate of Progress

All of it—your child's self-confidence, advancement in school, dollars-and-cents success in later life—depends overwhelmingly on the ability to learn, an ability to squeeze every ounce of power out of his or her brain that nature has built into it.

And that ability—today more than ever before—depends on YOU!

Is It Really That Hard to Get Top Grades? The Answer is NO

Once—perhaps fifteen years ago—the facts listed above might have added up to a life sentence of failure for the child who was having trouble with schoolwork, day after day.

Fifteen years ago, we might have believed that poor grades reflected a poor mind, that the student who did badly in class lacked either scholastic ability or intelligence.

We might have believed this fifteen years ago. But today, we realize that it's a myth.

Again, let's look at the facts.

Given average ability, students who do badly in school do badly because no one has ever taught them to study efficiently.

Without the proper study techniques, it is perfectly possible for students to get only HALF of the material needed in a lesson. Without the proper retention techniques, and without the proper test-taking techniques, it is possible for students to score only HALF the grade possible.

Schools can doom your child through negligence to struggling through school as a HALF-DOER.

Your child does not have to be brilliant to succeed either in school or in life. The only thing separating an average student from a fruitful scholastic life is DIRECTION—the ability to get the best possible results out of his or her own efforts. Remember the mind can actually become more powerful with the right structures.

Given this direction, anyone with average intelligence can maintain a superior school average. Every year, students who know how to study get grades far beyond those that might be expected from their IQ ability level. The difference is TECHNIQUE, pure and simple.

Technique . . . Direction . . . Guidance . . . Method! These are the secrets of success in school. Not an IQ! Not "inborn ability." Not some mysterious hidden talent that enables a few gifted students to solve problems at a glance that other students would never be able to understand, no matter how hard they worked on them.

This idea is pure nonsense. The real difference between the top student and the mediocre student lies not in ability, but in technique, and technique can be TAUGHT.

Because of this one simple fact—and because of the almost miraculous breakthroughs in the last few years about how the brain learns, there is no longer any reason to be forever catching up while classmates are going forward, to suffer the discouragement of being behind, to experience school as drudgery and disappointment, and to be branded forever as dull or slow-minded.

Studying is a skill, and it can be improved by practice like any other skill.

The ability to study can be improved drastically by learning a few simple ways to study scientifically. Learning research tells us that using as many senses as possible in studying leads to high achievement. Your child needs to practice techniques to see, hear, speak, and write information he or she is learning.

YOU can teach your child enough of these techniques in a week to start him or her on the road to doubling grades in school.

Here Is Exactly What the Book Will Do for You— and Your Child

This is the purpose of this book: To teach you how to double your child's grades in school with the least effort and in the shortest possible time. These techniques can advance students of all ages and ability, from those with learning disabilities to the very gifted.

I believe that next to loving your child this is the most important task you will ever be given as a parent. And next to love this is the greatest single gift you will ever give him or her.

But why YOU? Why should YOU have to teach your child these skills? Why not the teachers, in school?

Your child's teachers don't even have enough time to teach all the information he or she should know about a subject, let alone teach how to master this information. You have to work as a team with teachers to make sure your child knows these priceless study techniques, because schools are set up with the idea that your child already knows how to learn.

And for another very simple reason—overcrowding. Packed classrooms. Thirty or more children to a teacher. Not enough personal attention. Not enough explanation of difficult concepts and problems. Not enough individual drill.

This is the conclusion my own son's principal and I came to, in his very first grade in school. There is nothing in this book that conflicts in any way with what your child is being taught in school.

Exactly the opposite. The techniques in this book are designed to make the learning of that school material twice as easy and twice as fast, to make the absorption and mastery of that material almost automatic, to greatly relieve the teacher's burden by sending your child to class PREPARED to absorb information.

And what will these techniques do for your child? Simply this:

1. They will remove present study habits that make learning unpleasant and burdensome, and replace them with new, simpler, and easier habits that turn study into a soaring hour of achievement every time your child opens a book.
2. In other words, they will reduce effective study procedures to the habitual level. They will make them *a part of your child,* to get right down to the core of every lesson, automatically, the instant he or she opens a book.
3. Because of these new study habits, and sooner than you dare expect today, your child's ability to learn and to perform will zoom, will reveal such a change that teachers may actually call you to see what happened.
4. Study periods will shrink in time—sometimes actually in half—while the work turned out will double in quantity and quality.
5. And there will be no more forcing your child to study. Studying will suddenly become a privilege rather than a punishment, because each new lesson will give him or her a new taste of success, a new thrill of understanding, a stronger and stronger realization that he or she can conquer knowledge, owning it, day after day.
6. Therefore conduct in class will improve, as your child gets satisfaction from achievement, from performance, rather than frustrated rebellion. He or she will make new friends, better friends, like-minded "achievers," boys and girls who are really going places in this modern scientific and technological world of ours.
7. But above all, your child will be happier, because of doing something and finding success. This is the number one requirement for happiness in anything we do in life.
   And what of your child's grades? What will happen to the marks your child brings home—those magic percentage points that are the passports to college, scholarship, and the great world of achievement beyond? Simply this:
8. Your child's grades will double. Let me be perfectly clear on this point. His or her grades—if you apply these techniques—will actually double.

This means that if your child is now getting a C in a course, he or she will get a B. If your child is getting a B, he or she will get an A. If your child is now getting a D or below, the results may be even more dramatic.

If a student is graded by a percentage-point system rather than by letter, this doubling process will result in an improvement of about ten to fifteen points tacked on to the previous grades. Where your child had 70 before, he or she may now reach 80 or even 85. A score of 80 before may go as high as 95.

This dramatic jump in grades, produced over and over again, in test after test, will put your child in the advanced class he or she would have otherwise missed. It will give your child the ability to choose the college he or she wants, which might be otherwise barred. It may even bring in the scholarship you need to send him or her to one of the best schools in the country.

Isn't this worth one week's pleasant reading right now, and a few minutes' checking a day while your child is forging ahead?

That's all it takes. All the equipment you need is right here. These simple rules apply to anyone, at any level, in any grade.

To put them to work for YOUR CHILD—to carve out the life and success and achievement you want for YOUR CHILD—you start right here.

The Simple Strategy of Top Grades

HOW GOOD ARE YOUR CHILD'S STUDY HABITS?

• • •

Take This Three-Minute Test

Is your child living up to his or her full potential? Is your child squeezing out the absolute top grades that inborn intelligence will allow?

In other words, are your child's present study habits helping or hindering? Is the power of your child's brain being harnessed from the very first minute he or she opens a book—or blocked every step of the way?

This three-minute checklist will tell you right now. It is a quick, scientific rundown, not of your child's intelligence, but of the results his or her present study habits are capable of giving.

Simply observe your child studying for a single night. Then answer these questions with a yes or no. In three brief minutes, every weak spot in your child's study pattern will be thrown into the spotlight. You'll see the roadblocks in the way, and you'll take your first step toward removing them.

Ask yourself these questions and answer them coldly and honestly. Does your child:

- Have trouble finding studying materials?____
- Take hours to get going on homework?____
- Find it hard to focus on what he or she is studying?____
- Have trouble picking out the main points of the lesson he or she is reading?____
- Forget the next day what was read the night before?____
- Spend fruitless hours trying to figure out standard math problems?____
- Make the same mistakes over and over again?____
- Have difficulty expressing thoughts on paper?____
- Imitate other classmates' reports and essays, rather than create his or her own?____
- Forget vocabulary words almost as fast as he or she learns them?____
- Have a notebook that's a mess of scribbles, doodles and torn-up pages?____
- Never finish work on time?____
- Cram desperately for tests?____
- Become sick with fear before tests?____

How many questions did you answer with "yes"? If there was even one, this book will be worth far more to you and your child than the price you paid for it.

If you had four "yes" answers, then your child is losing over 25 percent of his or her brain power through sloppy study habits. In other words, your child is using at least 25 percent less brain power than his or her inborn ability should provide. This book will restore those lost percentage points.

And if you had eight or more "yes" answers, then your child is in trouble; you can see it at a glance, and you—and your child—are in for one of the most dramatic and painless improvement performances of your entire lives.

Save this test. Check your answers, in pen or pencil, on this page. Refer to each "yes" answer—to each weak point—as you reach the section that covers it in this book.

Then, one week from now, when you've finished this book, and you and your child have run through the methods described in its pages—at that point take this test again. Write down your new answers—one week from today—next to the old.

The difference may actually take your breath away. You can actually see your child grow, see study habits change in that first week, and see her or him turn the corner to success.

And if there are any "yes" answers left at the end of that first week—or at the end of the first big test—then simply mark those weak points. Run over the procedures again. And repeat the test one month later.

You'll see those "yes" answers evaporate like water on a hot stove. And you'll also see results of those procedures on the next report card, and on every report card, in every subject, that your child brings home from that day on.

HIGHER GRADES

OVERNIGHT

● ● ●

Our Plan of Attack for Higher Grades Overnight—
What You and Your Children Must Do

Parents of high-achieving students know the secret. They use a plan that follows proven methods. And the U.S. Department of Education verified these proven methods in the bulletin *What Works*.

After combing through thousands of studies on learning, the researchers found what many parents already knew: Parents who monitor their children's schoolwork have the most outstanding students—better than if the family were "well-off."

One such family I know has a daily routine for their children, who are on their school's honor roll. Every afternoon when the two children come home, they pass a bulletin board in the hallway. On that board they write a homework schedule.

That evening at dinner, their parents will ask them to talk about their reading and be able to give main ideas and details. And the children will have to give their own opinion. They will have to defend that opinion against others—and make that opinion stick.

Every night, the same priceless concern. Five minutes a day to instill brilliance and leadership into growing children, to give them all-important gifts.

1. The ability to read quickly and surely, and understand every word they read.
2. The ability to pick out the important details from a mass of words, and burn them indelibly into their minds.
3. The ability to express their own thoughts in their own words, and to express them quickly, powerfully, and convincingly.
4. The ability to reason, to think logically, to fill in unstated facts, to detect lies and errors, to project present events into the future, to persuade others to accept their point of view.

The Four All-Important Gifts

These gifts are worth far more to your children than vast fortunes. And they can be transmitted at no greater cost than five minutes a day of your time and direction.

That same five minutes a day you can give to your children to build success into their future. And it is the only cost, of either time or money, that this book asks of you.

Here is the reason why.

The Three Simple Building Blocks of Success

In the past few years, a great many educators have become confused. They have become so fascinated with the content of social studies, physics, foreign languages, and the like, that they have forgotten how simple a good education really is.

A good education—a bedrock education—an education upon which your children will either succeed or fail—*consists of just three simple skills.*

- The ability to read.
- The ability to express thoughts in words.
- The ability to solve mathematical problems.

The Three Building Blocks of Success

Reading, writing, and mathematics. Your grandparents knew it. We've forgotten it; and we have to get back to it.

These are the foundation stones. Everything else, all the advanced subjects, depends on them. For example, if you can't understand what you read, you can't read science. If you can't express your own thoughts, you can't write good reports. And if you can't solve basic problems in algebra, then you won't even be able to start on calculus or physics.

Everything your child does in future years depends upon the ability to read, to write, and to figure. For the rest of your child's life, he or she will be reading newspapers, memos, articles, and reports. Your child will be writing letters, applications, recommendations, e-mail, and progress reports. And your child will be figuring grocery bills, installment charges, mortgage payments, and profit and loss.

If your child can't read like an expert, write like an expert, and figure like an expert, then anything else you do for his or her mind will be wasted.

Therefore, your fundamental task—the one great secret of building success into your child—is to make absolutely sure that child is a "blooming genius" in reading, writing, and mathematics.

And I mean *genius!* When we get through with that child of yours, we're going to have classmates pop-eyed at his or her ability to read a printed page, to write a written report, or to cut through a mathematical problem to its very heart.

Your child will have your direct help and also a "To the Student" section at the end of each chapter to review the key points in each lesson on his or her own, again and again.

Reading, writing, and mathematics. You are going to make your child a master in each of these. And you are going to do it in five short minutes a day, using three incredibly powerful tools.

- Enthusiasm
- Praise
- A good, kind ear

The Three Powerful Tools

Here's how they combine to get your child off to a whiz-bang start—today.

It's What Your Child Can Put to Use That Counts

Your primary job, then, is twofold. First, you must teach your child the scientific techniques of reading, writing, and mathematics contained in this book.

Second, you must have your child put them to use, to recite them in front of you and sometimes the mirror, so you can make absolutely sure he or she has them right.

This is the one-two punch that shoots grades up overnight.

1. Use new scientific techniques of study.   **The One-Two**
2. Back them up with a daily parent   **Punch**
   checkup to see that your child is using
   them correctly.

In computer language, this checking-up process is called "feedback." Engineers know that it's not what you feed into a computer that counts; it's what the computer does with that information—what it "feeds back" to you—that counts. Some of that information can be lost, forgotten, or distorted. You have to ask for it again to make sure.

The same with your child. In every subject, for every day of school, what he or she reads means nothing. Words can simply pour in and out of your child's mind like water through a funnel. The only thing that counts is what sticks—how much your child understands and remembers and how much he or she can put to immediate use.

Burn this fact into your mind. To learn any subject, mere reading is only the first step. *The complete, effective learning process is made up of four steps.*

- Reading   **Four Steps of**
- Understanding   **Complete,**
- Remembering   **Effective**
- Reproducing in one's own   **Learning**
  thoughts and words

This is the goal you want for your child. Reproducing, putting to use, expressing in his or her own words, either on paper or in classroom recitation. (Or, in the case of mathematics, in solving new problems.)

This is what you are aiming for: the end result. If your child's learning process stops short of this goal, this effective self-expression, then that child is failing the study period and getting only half the benefit of his or her work.

You have to make sure your child gets it all. You have to check work every day. Here is how you do it.

The Five-Minute Daily Achievement Check

Starting today and continuing every day of your child's school career, do this:

You should spend at least five minutes a day with your child and his or her homework. The time of day is unimportant; but you must be able to give that time completely to your child, in full concentration upon his problems, with no interruptions and no sense of being hurried.

For these few minutes each day, nothing in the world matters but your child and the homework.

This is a recitation period, a discussion period, and eventually a "show-off" period. It should have the following schedule, and you should run through the entire schedule in this exact order, each day.

1. Examine the work he or she is going to turn in the next morning. See that handwritten work is neat and has no misspellings.

   The Five-Minute Achievement Check

2. See that work done on a word processor has been spell-checked and proofread.
3. Question what is not clear to you, and have your child explain it to you until you are sure he or she understands it.
4. Hear memory work.
5. Check mathematics work for obvious errors.

6. Check the assignment book to see that your child has completed all homework.

7. Now check the work received back from teachers. If it has errors on it, turn the paper over and ask your child to rework the problems on its back until he or she gets the correct answers. Every error must be redone correctly the same day it is handed back.

You have now completed the Achievement Check. At the beginning it will take more than five minutes. But soon your child will understand what is expected, and the work will improve. Your child will be prepared for the check. And you will zip through it with perhaps the warmest glow of pride you have known in years.

In every case, if your child's work does not meet your standards, then he or she must do it over again. And submit it again and again until it is right.

But your criticism of your child's work must be objective, calm, and sympathetic. There must be no punishment, no raised voices, no downgrading. You are there to help, and not humiliate. You must make it perfectly clear at every session that you know he or she can do the job, that these are only temporary setbacks, that you are looking forward to the day, with complete confidence, when your only reaction to your child's work will be undiminished praise.

And when that day comes, and for every tiny victory on the way to that day, make sure above all that you are lavish with that praise.

The Most Powerful Weapon You Have to Encourage Top Grades from Your Child

Let me emphasize this fact again:

Praise makes winners.

Encouragement—not criticism—builds success into those you are trying to help.

Enthusiasm is the magic ingredient that makes people perform miracles, that brings home results far beyond your fondest dreams.

Just visualize your child's world for a moment. Realize that a mathematics paper graded 100, or a perfect essay, is as important to your child as is a salary raise to you.

It takes as much struggle and effort for your child to learn to write a page of clear paragraphs as it does for you to prepare an entire advertising campaign, or strip down and refinish a piece of furniture, or plan and put into execution a community-wide charity drive.

The effort is exactly the same. And the feeling of accomplishment and pride is also the same. Therefore, when such accomplishment occurs—no matter how tiny it may seem to you—view it through your child's eyes and reward him or her accordingly.

In other words, make a large-scale fuss about very small accomplishments. And soon those accomplishments will grow very large indeed.

Always remember, your job is not only to implant skill in your child, but self-confidence as well. And self-confidence comes from only one source—admiration and praise. Accomplishment must be rewarded.

IN SUMMARY ....

Your child's entire education rests on mastering three bedrock skills.

- Reading
- Writing
- Mathematics

The Three Bedrock Skills

The purpose of this book is to help you improve those skills to the point of near-perfection. This is done in three ways.

1. By teaching your child new scientific techniques of learning how to learn.

The Keys to Skill Improvement

2. By checking back on your child's work every day to make sure he or she has understood these techniques and put them to use.

3. By having your child do his or her own
    review of each daily lesson.

The basic procedure therefore is this. All schoolwork papers—coming and going—must be brought to your attention and gone over carefully. All mistakes must be corrected, with neatness praised and success rewarded.

Through this simple procedure, your child will learn a respect for, and a striving toward, that most magic of all words—*excellence.*

We are striving in this book for excellence in your child.

And we begin by teaching a few simple tricks of organization, to help your child get twice as much done in half the time he or she spends today.

GET TWICE AS MUCH DONE

• • •

Organization: How to Do Twice as Much in Half the Time

Most students waste at least half their study time, because no one has ever shown them how to organize their work.

This is the purpose of this chapter—to cut the waste out of your child's study, and make sure he or she gets a full minute's results for every minute spent studying.

What Is Organization?

Organization is simply *planned direction*. It is a procedure. A system. A planned schedule of events or tasks, one after the other, that gets something done in the shortest possible time, with the least amount of waste.

It is doing the right thing at the right time. And not wasting your time doing the wrong thing.

In your child's schoolwork, therefore, organization can be reduced to seven steps or keys.

- Sitting down at a desk.
- Finding out what has to be done.
- Opening the right book to the right page to do it.
- Starting to do it at the beginning.
- Learning it step by step.
- Knowing when it is finished and when it is right.
- And then remembering what it is he or she has learned, how he or she has studied, and how he or she will use this knowledge tomorrow.

The Seven Keys to Organization

Without such a definite step-by-step plan of attack, your child will waste time by not getting down to work immediately. Your child will not be sure exactly what it is he or she is supposed to learn and will wander aimlessly until stumbling on what needs to be done. Then your child may lose it again, or waste time on any number of distractions, or forget it before class the next day.

The most beautiful thing about organization is that it is *far simpler and far easier* than what your child is doing today. It not only gives higher grades—instantly—but it does it with far less study time.

And it's so easy to put into practice. All the organization your child needs can be broken down into two simple formulas.

The Essence of All Organization

1. Getting down to work
2. Doing the work right

Let's look at each of them in turn.

No More Crises, No More Fear

Any subject becomes easy if you organize it on a long-term basis, day by day, lesson by lesson and step by step. Constant, daily study

Organization Makes Anything Easy

periods, therefore, are the first magic keys to success.

The first step in organizing your child's study habits is to set up a daily work schedule and make sure you both stick to it.

Set Up a Daily Work Schedule First

There is just no substitute for regular daily study—for a certain amount of time spent daily on each subject. Life as a student becomes incredibly easy if your child maintains a steady pace from start to finish of the school year. Then there are no sudden pressures to get things done. No near-hysteria about deadlines. No tensions and anxieties in class.

There Is No Substitute for Daily Study

With a daily work schedule, religiously enforced, all these crises are miraculously replaced by the wonderfully secure feeling of being adequately prepared. This, in turn, leads to a steady, comforting flow of high marks.

Be Secure

Here's a Sample Daily Work Schedule

Let's look at such a daily schedule, and see how simple it is to set up and how easy it is to follow.

Your Child's Daily Achievement Schedule

Monday through Friday

6:30 A.M.	Wake up
6:30–6:45	Wash and dress
6:45–7:00	Breakfast
6:45–7:00	Help around the house
7:00–7:10	Final preparation for school
7:10–7:40	Go to school
7:40–8:00	Pre-school talk with friends

8:00–2:45 P.M.	Regular class schedule
2:45–3:15	Go home from school
3:15–5:15	Recreation, practice, and so on
5:15–5:45	Help in house and wash up
5:45–6:30	Dinner
6:30–7:00	Help with cleanup
7:00–7:15	*Prepare for study time— get all materials together*
7:15–8:00	*Study*
8:00–8:05	*Parent check on homework*
8:05–8:15	Break
8:15–9:00	*Study*
9:00–10:00	Break
10:00–10:15	Prepare for bed
10:15–6:30 A.M.	Sleep

Start the Week Off Right on Sunday Night

Weekends are basically free for relaxing, sports, socializing, and other interests; but Sunday night should include study time.

Your Child's Weekend Achievement Schedule

Saturday	Free day
Sunday	Free until 7:00 P.M.
7:00–8:00 P.M.	*Study*
8:00–8:05	Parent check
8:05–8:15	Break
8:15–9:15	*Study*
9:15–10:00	Break
10:00–10:15	Prepare for bed
10:15–6:30 A.M.	Sleep

The exact details in this schedule are, of course, merely suggestions. Your own family activities may dictate different dinner hours, relaxation breaks, parent checks, and so on. And, of course, as your child enters high school, and beyond, the study period will have to be lengthened to two hours or more each night.

But the important points are clear. Every day—every single day—there must be at least one hour and a half for study and five minutes for recitation—without exception. Without excuse. Without delay!

This study period is essential to your child's career. It is as vital to his or her future as your work is to yours. *It must start at exactly the same time each night, without delay. And it must be followed by a careful, concentrated check before that child can close his or her books and go on to something else.*

Let's take a closer look at that daily study period and see how we can make it produce twice the results for your child.

Tips That Double the Value of Each Study Period

Your child will not do top work in the study period unless you make that study period as important to you as it is to her or him. This means:

1. Your child must have a definite place to study. It must be his or her place. The same place each night, with no one else having any claim to it for that time period.

   How to Double the Value of Every Study Period

2. It must be comfortable and bright, with the physical equipment to read and write permanently stored there, instantly at hand when needed.

3. There must be no distractions for that hour and a half. This means, ideally, his or her room with the door closed. No radio, TV, or music. No interruptions. No friends working with him. No phone calls for any reason. When your child begins to work, he or she stays at work until finishing.

   If your child does not have his or her

own room, then you must provide the exclusive use of one adequate space for that hour and a half. This means no other members of the family around, conversing or rustling newspapers. Your child needs silence to concentrate. And you have to make whatever sacrifices are necessary to provide a quiet area.

4. But this ruling out of distractions goes one step further. It also means that your child has, at study time, only the equipment needed and nothing more: No unnecessary books. No newspapers. No clutter to draw attention away. Studying is business—all business.

5. Make sure your child starts lessons at the same exact moment every day. A five-minute delay can kill an entire study period. The phone conversation is cut off, and he or she is at the desk at the precise moment when scheduled.

6. You are setting up a *routine,* a constant, daily psychological readiness to study. An automatic ability to concentrate can only come from getting down to work at the same time, in the same spot, every day. Once this routine is established, waste motion is eliminated and work flashes by. At the end of that period, when you are ready to review that work, you will be delighted at the quantity and quality of it.

7. Organize your child's study materials. In addition to creating an environment that will increase the value of your child's study hours, you must help your child organize his or her study materials.

8. Establish a separate notebook section for each course. Your child's teacher will probably recommend a system of note-taking. If the teacher does not, what works for many students is a large, 3-ring, looseleaf notebook with a separator tab for each course. This notebook can be referred to as "course notes" also. Whatever type of notebook a student uses, he or she should write on only one side of each page, reserving the back of the page for future corrections or additions.

IN SUMMARY ....

Organization is planned direction. It is the ability to:

1. Get down to work without wasted motion.
2. Get the work done right.

In this chapter we have seen that organization makes even the hardest subjects easy by attacking them day after day.

In order to do this, a definite study period must be set aside every day, at exactly the same time, in exactly the same spot, with exactly the same equipment. Study materials must be organized and easily gotten.

Once this routine is established, getting down to work becomes instant and automatic. Your child is ready to slash into work without a second's wasted motion.

To the Student: Do It Yourself

- Set up a study schedule.
- Organize your work area so there are no distractions.
- Set up a file system.
- Organize your study materials and supplies.

Now let's teach your child the second part of organization: How to fill up that study period with achievement—how to do that work right.

You will start with the basic art of reading—how to cut through reading assignments in half your child's present time, with an absolute understanding of every word.

Digging Out the Facts— Reading

WORD POWER FOR YOUR CHILD

• • •

Including Understanding New Words Without a Dictionary

The first requirement to be a good reader is *a mastery of words.*

As your child reads, as he or she listens and gains information from any source whatever, *your child learns new words.*

This word learning is one of the most important parts of your child's education. For words are the tools of thought—mental tools that make thought far easier, far more exact, and far more powerful in solving the problems he or she will encounter in later life.

Your child will actually get smarter. The more he or she learns, the more mental tools he or she will have to earn higher scores on standardized tests. Each word added will develop more mind connections to new information. The purpose of this chapter is to show you how to help your child master these tools.

How to Build Word Power Early

What is the proper age to actively teach your child new words—to deliberately expand his or her vocabulary? At the very latest, by the time your child is in first grade. It is so easy to do, and so much fun, that it makes one of the most entertaining and profitable parent and child games ever invented. Here's how it goes.

One night, at the dinner table, take a sentence out of your child's first reading book. For example: "The dog could not climb the green tree." Take a phrase out of that sentence, for example, "the green tree."

And then begin to explore with your child other words that might be found with "tree." Open up whole new realms of existence, simply by substituting one word for another, like this:

"Are there many green *trees* in your city block?" Probably not.

"Then let's take a mental trip outside the city to the fields where you and your friends can run and play.

"Just beyond those fields is the edge of a wood, with many trees, and that wood is also called a *grove*.

"If the wood is thick enough and reaches far enough, so that we might easily get lost in it if we go too far, we call it a *forest*.

"And, finally, if it is far south, where it is very warm, and the trees are thick and soggy, and there are strange and dangerous animals lurking everywhere, we call it a jungle.

So you see how even as simple a word as "tree," to children who are no older than five or six, can grow in pictures and feelings. Wonderful new worlds of adventure can be opened up. You can make your child's storehouse of words expand and expand.

But how many of these new words has your child retained? Now you find out by asking questions like these:

"What is a *grove?*"

If a *wood* is so big that it covers hills and valleys and mountains and lakes, what is it called?

"Where are *jungles* found?"

And so on, until each of these new words becomes second nature, until you can fairly see his or her vocabulary stretch and grow before your very eyes.

How to Make Your Child's Recitations Sparkle

Later, when your child becomes eight or nine years old, you make the game still more interesting. Now it becomes the Change-the-

Word Game—a search for substitute words in a story, to see what magic changes he or she can make when fitting words into stories.

For example, take the magnificent line from the Old Testament: "When they were in the field, Cain rose up against Abel and slew him." What would happen if we changed the key words in this sentence? Would we make the sentence better? Would we add or subtract meaning? Ask your child to try it and see.

Perhaps the two of you will replace "rose up against" with such words as "conspired against," "blindly hated," "treacherously attacked."

Perhaps you will replace "slew" with such words as "killed," "murdered," "butchered," or "assassinated."

Which of these new words is the most exciting? Which carries the thought best?

As you play on, your child learns to search for exactly the right word to project the color and meaning of what he or she wants to say. Your child feels at home with all kinds of words—small and large, simple and exotic. Your child adds drama and depth to everything he or she says or writes. And you see the difference almost immediately in your child's grades.

How to Teach Your Child to Identify Strange Words, Without Looking Them Up

Still later, at ten or eleven, your child will be ready to play the most thrilling and profitable game of all—learning how words are built and how to recognize new words without having to interrupt reading to look them up.

This also can be made an adventure in learning, if you follow this simple, two-step plan.

First of all, show your child that all words are built up, part by part, just as a model airplane is.

Words, however, are much simpler. They have just these three basic parts.

1. They have a root or stem, which gives the basic meaning, such as "go." **The Three Parts of Words**

2. Then there is the *front part,* or *prefix,* which adds another meaning to the root word, such as "out" plus "go" equals "outgo."

3. And then there is the end part, or suffix, which gives still another meaning. For example, "-ing," which rounds out our word to make "out" plus "go" plus "ing" add up to "outgoing."

Thus we can build one big word out of three small ones. And this gives us a brand-new word that is much easier to remember, takes far less space to write, and actually represents a new meaning that we would not have had with the three smaller words at all.

This is the way language grows: by taking two or three small words, and building a new word out of them. And, by doing it, giving us new meanings to solve new problems.

There are *three* basic building blocks, then, to build new words—the *root,* the *front part,* and the *end part.*

Some words have only the root, like "hear." Other words have only the root and the end part, like "hearing." Still others have only the root and a front part, like "unheard," and others have all three parts, like "unhearing."

Now, how does this knowledge help your child recognize strange words without looking them up? In a very simple way.

Most big words that your child doesn't recognize are actually made up of smaller words, in exactly the manner we have just described. They are made up of the same three basic building blocks we've just examined.

However, many of these smaller word parts are in Latin, for the very simple reason that Latin was the ancient language that was a parent language of present-day English. Also, many words have their origins in the Greek language.

Therefore, in order to work out the meaning of a strange word the first time your child sees it, all he or she has to do is learn these Latin and Greek word parts, and see how they fit together to make new words.

The Most Profitable Word Game Your Child Will Ever Play

Listed below are some of the most common Latin and Greek word parts in our language. It has been said that from a mere twelve of these parts, we have built over 2,500 English words. *No wonder it pays your child dividends to learn one or two of them every night.*

Let's start with the most common *front parts*, or *prefixes*. Here's the *front part* itself, what it means, and a common English word that uses it. Notice how easy the word is to understand at a glance, once you know the meaning of the *front part*.

Common Latin and Greek Prefixes

Front Part	Meaning	Common Word
a, au	not, without	atypical
ab, abs	to free from	absolve
ad	to	adhere
am, amb, ambi	about, around, both	ambiguous
amphi	both, around	amphibious
ante	before	anteroom
ant, anth, anti	opposed to	anti-labor
arch, archi	chief, principal	archbishop
aut, auth, auto	self	automatic
bi, bis	two, double	biennial
caco	bad, ill	cacophonous
cata	down, complete	catalogue
circum	around	circumference
col, com, con, cor	jointly	combine
contra, contro	against	contradict
counter	in opposition to	counteract
de	from, down	deduce
di, dis	away from	dismiss
dia	between	dialogue
en	in, into	energetic
ep, eph, epi	upon, on, over	epitaph
equi	equal	equidistant

Common Latin and Greek Prefixes *(continued)*

Front Part	Meaning	Common Word
eu	well, good	euphony
ex, e	out	exit
extra	beyond, outside of	extraordinary
hetero	another, different	heterogeneous
hyper	over	hypercritical
hypo	under, below	hypodermic
i, il, im, in, ir, ig	not	inept, ignoble
inter	between	interstate
intra	within	intrastate
intro	place before	introduce
mal, male	bad	malpractice
meta	after, change	metaphor
mis	wrong	mislabel
miso	hatred of	misogyny
mono	one, alone	monologue
multi	many	multiply
neo	new	neophyte
non	not	nonsense
ob	against	obstruct
ortho	correct, right	orthoptic
pan	all	panacea
para	beside	parallel
per	through	permit
peri	around	perimeter
poly	many	polygon
post	after	postscript
pre	before	prejudge
pro	before	pronoun
proto	first	protocol
pseudo	false, fictitious	pseudonym
psycho	relating to mind or soul	psychology
re, red	back, again	redo, reincarnation
retro	backward, back	retroactive, retrospect

Common Latin and Greek Prefixes *(continued)*

Front Part	Meaning	Common Word
se, sed	away, aside, apart	secede
semi	half	semi-circle
sub	under	submarine
super	above	superabundant
syn, sy	together	syntax
trans, tra	through, across	transport
tri	three	triangle
ultra	excessive	ultra-sweet
un, uni	one	uniform

Now for *end parts*, or *suffixes*. Notice how they, too, add to the meaning of every word they touch.

Common Latin and Greek Suffixes

End Part	Meaning	Common Word
able, ible	able to be	believable
age	state of being	marriage
al	belonging to	constitutional
an, ave	belonging to	Georgian
an, ain	a member of	Republican
ance	quality	tolerance
ancy, ency	quality or state of	clemency
ant, ent,	one who does	servant
ar	relating to	angular
ard, art	one who does	coward
ary	engaged in	secretary
ate	to make	animate
ation	the act of	dedication
cy	practice of	democracy
dom	state of	martyrdom
ee	one who receives	assignee
eer	one who is engaged in	volunteer
en	to make	moisten

Common Latin and Greek Suffixes *(continued)*

End Part	Meaning	Common Word
ern	belonging to	western
er	one who does	miner
er	belonging	Marylander
ery	occupation	surgery
esque	like, style of	statuesque
ferous	bearing, giving	auriferous
fold	number	twofold
ful	full of	resentful
gram	a writing	telegram
graph	a writing	autograph
hood	state of	brotherhood
ial	pertaining to	editorial
ic, ical	resembling	fantastic
ice	act, quality	justice
ify	to make	gratify
il, ile	capable of being	versatile
ine	of the nature of	canine
ion	the act of	decision
ious	full of	ambitious
ish	characteristic of	bookish
ism	belief or theory	racism
ist	one who practices	florist
ity	quality of	acidity
ive	tending to	abusive
ize	to follow an action	economize
less	lacking	useless
ling, long	showing direction	headlong
logy	science of	geology
ly	having qualities of	friendly
ment	act or process of	investment
ness	a quality	happiness
ogy	study of	geology
or	one who does	tailor
ory	of	prohibitory

Common Latin and Greek Suffixes *(continued)*

End Part	Meaning	Common Word
ose	containing	verbose
ous	full of	mountainous
ry	practice of	chemistry
sion	the act of	ascension
tion	the act of	inspection
trix	feminine agent	executrix
tude	state of	rectitude
ty	practice of	fidelity
ure	act of	rapture
vorous	feeding on	carnivorous
ward	direction of	eastward
wise	way of	clockwise
wright	maker	playwright
y, ey	pertaining to	smoky

Now the *root words* (or base meanings) themselves. There are, of course, hundreds of them. All we can do is list some of the most common here. If your child wishes to learn more of them, he or she can easily find them in any good book on word building.

Again, notice how seemingly hard words become a cinch to understand when your child recognizes their word parts. And also notice how the *front* and *end* parts also build up the meaning of each word.

Common Latin and Greek Word Roots

Root Word	Meaning	Common Word
acer, acr	sharp	acerbity
ag, act, ig	carry on	agency
ali	nourish	alimentary
ali, allo, alle	other	alias
alter	another	alter
alt	high	altitude
ambul	walk	amble, ambulatory

Common Latin and Greek Word Roots *(continued)*

Root Word	Meaning	Common Word
am, em	friend	amicable
amo, ama	love	amorous
anim	life	animation
annu, enni	year	annual
anthrop	man	anthropology
appe	a call upon	appeal
aqua, aque	water	aquatic
arbiter	a judge	arbitration
art	art	artistic
ast, astr	star	astrology
audi, aur, aus	hear	audible
bell	hostile	rebellious
bible	book	bibliography
bio	life	biology
brevi	short	abbreviate
cad, cas, cid	fall	cadence
cam, chamb	room	chamber
camp, champ	country	campus
cant, chant, cent	sing	cantata
ced, cess, ceed	go	recede
celer	speed	accelerate
cent	hundred	century
chief, cap	head	captain
cap, capt	take, seize	capture
chrom, chromo, chroma	color	panchromatic
chron, chrono	time	synchronize
cide, cis, cise	cut, kill	suicide, scissors
cit	arouse	excite
civ, civi	citizen	civic
clam, claim	shout	clamor
clud, cluse	close, shut off	exclude
cline	bend	recline
coc, coct	cook	concoct
col, cul	till	cultivate

Common Latin and Greek Word Roots *(continued)*

Root Word	Meaning	Common Word
cor, cord	hear	accord
corp, corps, corpor	body	corporation
cras	tomorrow	procrastinate
cred, creed	believe	incredible
crea	create	creation
cresc, crue, cret, crete	grow	increase
crux, cruc	a cross	crucifix
crypt	hide	cryptogram
culp	blame	culpable
cur, course	to run	concurrent
cur, cura	care	curate
cycl	wheel	cycle
deca, deci	ten	decade
dem, demo	people	democracy
dens	thick	dense
derm	skin	dermatologist
dexter	right-handed	dexterity
di, dia	day	diary
dic, dict	speak	dictate
dign	worthy	dignitary
doc, doct	teach	doctrine
dom	master	dominate
dom	house	domestic
dorm	sleep	dormitory
du	two	duet
dur	hard, lasting	durable
duc, duct	lead	educate
dynam	power	dynamic
err	wander, go astray	errant
erg	work	energy
ego	I	egotist
fac	do	factory
fer	carry	transfer
ferv	boil	fervent

Common Latin and Greek Word Roots *(continued)*

Root Word	Meaning	Common Word
fid	faith, trust	fidelity
fil	son	filial
fin	limit	final
firm	strengthen	affirm
flex, flect	bend	flexible
flu, flux	flow	fluent
fort	strong	fortress
found, fuse, fund	pour	refund
fract, frang	break	fragile
frater	brother	fraternity
fug	flee	fugitive
gam	marriage	bigamist
geo	earth	geography
gen	birth	gender
gest, ger	carry, bear	gestation
gov, gub	govern, rule	government
grad, gress	walk, go	progress
grand	great	grandeur
graph	write	autograph
grat	pleasing, agreeable	gratitude
grav	heavy	gravity
greg	crowd	congregate
hab, hib	have, hold	habit
homos	same	homonym
hydr	water	hydrant
ject	throw	reject
jud	right	judgment
junct, jug	join	junction
juven	young	juvenile
labor	toil, work	laboratory
laud	praise	laudatory
lav	wash, clean	lavatory
leg, lig, lect	read, choose	legible
leg	law	legislature

Common Latin and Greek Word Roots *(continued)*

Root Word	Meaning	Common Word
lib	book	library
liber	free	liberty
lig	bind	oblige
liter	letter	literal
loc	place	location
locu, loqu	speak, talk	elocution
log	word	dialogue
luc, lum	light	illuminate
lud, lus	play	allude
magn	great	magnify
mand	order	mandate
man, manu	hand	manual
mar, mari	sea	maritime
mater	mother	maternal
matur	ripe	mature
med	middle	median
men, ment	mind	mentor
mens, mest	month	semester
merg	dip	submerge
meter	measure	diameter
mis, mit	send	permit
mon	advise	admonish
morph	shape	amorphous
mor, mort	death	mortal
mov, mot, mob	move	remove
mut	change	mutant
nasc, nat	born	nativity
nihil	nothing	annihilate
nom, nomin	name	nominate
nov	new	novice
nym	name	pseudonym
oper, opus	work	operator
path	feeling	sympathy
pater, patr	father	paternal

Common Latin and Greek Word Roots *(continued)*

Root Word	Meaning	Common Word
parl	talk	parliament
pars, part	a part	partner
ped, pod	foot	pedal
pel, puls	drive	impulse
pend, pens	hang, weigh	impending
pet	seek, ask	petition
pet, petr	rock	petrify
omni	all	omnibus
phil	love	philosophy
phobia	fear	hydrophobia
phon	sound	telephone
plic	twist	complicate
poli	city, state	political
port	carry	portable
pon, pos	put, place	exponent
pot	power	potentate
prim	first	primary
pris, prehen	seize, grasp	apprehend
prob	test	probation
put	think	compute
pyr	fire	pyromaniac
rog	question	interrogation
reg, rec	direct	direct
rupt	break	rupture
sci, scio	know	conscience
scop	watch	telescope
scrib, script	write	describe
seg, sect	cut	section
sed, ses, sid	seat	session
sens, sent	feel	sentiment
sequ, secu, sue	follow	sequence
sign	sign, mark	designate
sol	alone	solitude
solv, solu	loosen, free	absolve

Common Latin and Greek Word Roots *(continued)*

Root Word	Meaning	Common Word
somin	sleep	insomnia
soph	wise, wisdom	sophomore
spec, spect, spic	look, see	spectacle
spir, spirit	breathe	aspire
sta, sti, sist	stand	circumstance
stead	place	steadfast
strict	bind	district
stru	build	structure
tact, ting	touch	tactile
tail	cut	curtail
tang	touch	tangible
tend	extend	extend
tena, tain	hold	detain
tent, tempt	try	attempt
term	end, limit	terminal
terr, ter	earth	inter
tele	afar	telescope
theo	God	theology
therm	heat	thermometer
thesis	setting, statement	thesis
tor, tort	twist	distort
tract	draw	tractor
trib	pay, grant	tribute
typ	model	typical
umbr	shadow	umbrella
urb	city	urban
val	strength	validity
ven, vent	come	convene
ver	true	veracity
vert, vers, verse	turn	divert
via, voy, vio	way	convey
vinc, vict	conquer	victor
vir	man	virile
voc	call	vocation

Common Latin and Greek Word Roots *(continued)*

Root Word	Meaning	Common Word
vol	wish	voluntary
volu, volv, volt	turn, roll	involve
zoo	animal	zoology

And, of course, many more. Your child should have a Word Part page in the back of each subject's notebook section. Every time your child discovers a new word part, and learns its meaning, he or she should immediately write it down on the Word Part page for permanent reference. And, at the same time, he or she should see how many different words use this part to build their meaning. This is easily one of the most fascinating and profitable word games your child will ever play.

Two Dictionaries Every Child Should Own

To look up these word parts, and to give the meaning of every new word your child should come across in homework, he or she should own a dictionary. This can be any of the good pocket dictionaries on the market until senior high school or college. And then it should be a college dictionary. It will be one of the most used books in your child's entire library.

In addition to this personally owned reference dictionary, students should build up a special technical dictionary for every course. In every new course, especially in high school and college years, they will have to master the *fundamental vocabulary* for that course.

For example, even in grammar, students will have to know the meaning of *noun, pronoun, verb, adjective, adverb, preposition, participle, gerund,* and dozens more. Special words like these are often defined only once in a textbook—the first time they are introduced—and then are used over and over again throughout the textbook without being defined again. Often your child will forget their meaning in the interval, and be hopelessly lost in an advanced lesson.

This can easily be avoided by having your child set up a vocabulary page in the back of each course section of the notebook. Here, each time your child encounters a new word, he or she simply writes it down on this page, along with its precise definition. Then, when your child comes across it again in reading, he or she can simply look it up on the vocabulary page without loss of time or motion.

Remember, your child cannot understand a lesson without completely understanding the meaning of every word in that lesson.

Therefore it's up to you to make sure he or she masters each one of those words. Go over the vocabulary page with your child every night. Make her or him tell you about every new word learned during the day's studies. Make sure he or she knows how to spell it; how to pronounce it; how to use it in a sentence; and how to define it in the shortest possible number of words. Only then does your child have that word firmly fixed in mind, ready to go to work on the reading he or she is going to do tomorrow.

IN SUMMARY ....

Words are incredibly powerful mental tools that help your child solve problems. It has been found that the more successful the person—child or adult—the larger the vocabulary.

Therefore you must help your child master the words he or she will need for success. This can be easily done, in these three ways:

1. By helping your child develop the habit of searching for the exact right word—to enlarge vocabulary to give color and power to every sentence he or she speaks or writes.   **The Three Ways to Master Words**

2. By teaching your child the Latin and Greek word parts that help make up modern English language, and thus enabling her or him to recognize hundreds of strange new words at a glance, without having to interrupt reading to look them up immediately in a dictionary.

3.   By having your child build a personal fundamental vocabulary dictionary for every course. Thus he or she will gain a complete mastery of the language of that course, gain a deeper understanding of its way of thought, and cut hours of study time from the effort it takes to master it.

To the Student: Do It Yourself

- Study the Latin and Greek word parts, including front, end and root word parts.
- Have Word Part pages in the back of your course notebooks; include word parts and their meanings for reference.
- Make sure you have your own standard dictionary to look up new words when you study.
- Keep a personal fundamental vocabulary dictionary, including all special technical words for every course.

We now put these newly learned words to use in your child's reading and writing. We begin with reading.

HOW TO BECOME
A MASTER READER

• • •

A Few Easy Steps to
Better Reading Skills

The fundamental skill required for all education is reading.

The ability of your child to study effectively, to get top grades in any subject, depends almost entirely on the ability to read thoroughly and with understanding—on the ability to pull facts out of a printed page and make them his or her own.

Even in mathematics, your child must first read the instructions and then understand precisely what to do to solve each of the problems.

If your child cannot do this, cannot read any assignment with complete confidence and understanding, then he or she will go through the rest of school life suffering from two crippling handicaps.

1. Your child will be forever doing unneces- **Two Crippling**
   sary work. Every assignment will become **Handicaps**
   doubly difficult—read over and over again
   two or more times, with each sentence

painfully spelled out and only partially understood.

2. Your child will be forever making unnecessary mistakes. Teachers acknowledge that almost as many errors are made in homework and tests *through sheer misreading or misunderstanding of instructions as through lack of knowledge.*

Why burden your child for the rest of his or her life with this double waste? Especially when effective reading—active, aggressive reading that tears knowledge out of the printed page and burns it into your child's memory for good—is far easier and far faster than the word-by-word reading most children do today.

Here's why.

Good Reading Is Far More Than Merely Recognizing Words

We will assume in this book that your child already reads. In other words, that he or she can take the letters *c-a-t* and put them together to form the word "cat." And can take several such words and read them in the sentence, "The cat chases the mouse."

This, really, is what we usually mean when we speak of the activity "reading." That your child can mechanically scan a printed page and put the words together from that page to form sentences.

In turn, this mechanical reading, by some magic process, is supposed to put knowledge in your child's mind. According to this theory, once students have read a sentence or a series of sentences, the thought contained in them is supposed to be automatically transferred into memory.

This is nonsense. Absolute nonsense. Every parent, at one time or another, has seen his or her child read an entire page, and then not be able to remember a single fact from it five minutes later.

Mere mechanical reading is not enough. Passive reading is not enough. The ability to run your eye over a printed page—to make words out of the print on that page and put them together into sentences—*is only the beginning of Effective Reading.*

Effective Reading is far more than this.

Effective Reading goes one step beyond mere words.

Effective reading is the art of taking those words, and boiling them down into THOUGHTS. Of boiling down dozens, and even hundreds, of those words into ONE VITAL THOUGHT.

Of searching for the "guts" of an assignment—the two or three really important thoughts that it contains—and separating them from all the waste words and unnecessary details that surround them.

And then burning those few vital thoughts into your memory, so you can never forget them.

Good Reading Is a Search for Big Ideas

Let me repeat these all-important facts. Your child must be trained, not merely to read for words, but for *central thoughts.*

Your child must be taught that good reading is an active, aggressive search that has three steps.

1. Locating a main idea in the mass of words that contain it.
2. Separating that idea from its unnecessary details.
3. Boiling that idea down into a few easily remembered words.

The Three Steps to Active Reading

Your child becomes a good reader, therefore, only when he or she masters this technique of searching and boiling down. Searching and boiling down. Searching and boiling down.

Until he or she has taken the entire assignment—hundreds upon hundreds of words, sentences and paragraphs—and reduced them to a few vital thoughts that contain the meaning of them all, that sum up the meaning of them all.

And that can be burned into your child's memory forever in a few short moments. Ready to be put to use—to solve new problems or to answer questions in an examination—the very instant he or she needs them.

This Is a New Way to Read—Twice as Fast, Five Times as Effective

The rest of Part Two will be devoted to teaching reading this new way. It is surprisingly easy to learn. And it is far easier and far faster than your child's present method.

Let me outline right now what each of the following chapters is going to teach your child.

There are three easy steps to this new reading process. Each of the next three chapters explains one of them.

Chapters 6 to 8 show your child how to set up the search for big ideas: How to glance over assignments, in one or two short minutes, and locate each important thought, *before* he or she begins to read.

Chapter 9 shows how to power-read. How to flash through page after page, pulling out and marking down those important thoughts, merely glancing over their unnecessary details, and finishing with the assignment in half the time it has taken before.

Chapter 10 shows how to boil these vital thoughts down into a few words, and burn them into memory with the very same action.

And Chapter 11 shows how to use the same three-step technique in class, when your child is listening to a lecture. It enables your child to understand and remember what he or she *hears* equally as well as what he or she *reads*.

When your child has finished this section and put its simple methods to use, he or she will be a confident, accomplished reader who will be able to read any assignment that is given, easily, swiftly, and without fear. Your child will understand each word in an instant. And your child will remember the vital points of everything that's read and be able to put them to immediate use.

✎ IN SUMMARY ···

Good reading is far more than merely recognizing the meaning of words.

Good reading is an active, aggressive search for the *major thoughts* that are contained in these words.

This search has three steps.

1. Locating the main ideas.
2. Separating them from their unnecessary details.
3. Boiling them down into a few words that you can easily memorize.

How to Find the Major Thoughts in Words

To the Student: Do It Yourself

- Search for the main thoughts or main ideas in each reading assignment.
- When you find the main ideas, separate them from unnecessary details.
- Then boil down the main ideas into a few of your own words that you can easily memorize.

Now let's put these three steps into action. Let's examine each of these techniques in detail, along with concrete examples of what they will accomplish for your child.

HOW TO PRE-READ
A LESSON

• • •

Understand Before You Read

Let us suppose that a student is given a reading assignment in school. For example, he or she is told to read Chapter 6 in a history book on the Civil War. Or the next five pages on fractions in a math text. Or perhaps even a complete book report on *The Red Badge of Courage* by Stephen Crane.

Your child takes the book home. He or she sits down at the desk at the exact moment the evening study hour begins, and opens the book to the page assigned.

What does your child do now?

If your child simply begins to read the first words he or she sees—plunging right into that text without making any further preparation—then your child is making a crucial mistake that will cost hours of wasted effort every week, and that may cause him or her to miss the entire point of each lesson.

No one—no matter how bright—can really understand an assignment by simply beginning to read it word after word. It's like trying to drive to a destination by simply taking the first highway you see, without getting directions or looking at a road map.

Your child's first job in reading is to get those directions: to build that road map. To know exactly what to get out of that lesson. And where it's located.

To do this, your child pre-reads that lesson. He or she glances over that lesson from beginning to end—before starting to read—and picks out the following information.

1. *What's the main theme of this lesson?* (For example, the Civil War.)
2. *How much information does this lesson cover?* (The period from 1861 to 1864.)
3. *What are the* main thoughts *in this lesson that I have to remember?* (The crucial battles that turned the tide of the war.)
4. *How many of these* main thoughts *are there?* (About five or six.)
5. *What do I have to remember about each one of these* main thoughts? (The outcome of each battle.)
6. *Where in the lesson do I find this information?* (Now your child begins to read.)

The Six Essentials of Pre-Reading

Just Look at the Difference These Few Questions Make

Now, what exactly has happened here? Your child has invested one or two brief minutes to glance over the lesson from beginning to end. In that short time, he or she has picked out its main theme and each of its central thoughts. Your child has built a skeleton of that lesson—an outline of that lesson—a road map of that lesson to follow while reading.

Now your child knows what he or she is looking for. Now your child is walking a lighted path instead of stumbling in the dark. Now, instead of facing a confused jumble of words, your child slashes through that lesson with this definite purpose in mind:

What do I have to remember about each one of my main

thoughts? (What was the outcome of each battle in this history lesson?)

Now your child reads to answer this question. Your child has *direction.* In one or two minutes, your child has a better grasp of that assignment than if he or she reads it aimlessly for a full hour.

How to Find These Main Thoughts: Signposts That Point Them Out

Fortunately, the authors of your child's books agree with this road-map idea. They too believe in building an outline of the important thoughts in each lesson, and then simply filling in the details.

In order to help students do this, authors have built into their books certain signposts that point out these main thoughts. These signposts stick out from the main body of the text. They are the chapter headings, section headings, table of contents, summary paragraphs, and all other vital points set off by capital letters, underlining, italics and other attention-drawing devices.

They form a book within a book. And by learning how to read them, your child can pick out the main points of that book almost as fast as he or she can turn its pages.

Let's teach your child how to really use them, right now. Let's start with the big signposts, the ones needed the very first time he or she picks up a book—the ones that will give the guts of that entire book in five to ten minutes.

And then let's work our way down to the smaller signposts, the ones that will organize your child's study each time he or she has another assignment in that book.

For the first few examples, we'll use this book—the one you're reading now. This will give you a chance to check your own reading habits, to see if you're getting as much information out of each page as you should.

Then we'll go on to examples from standard textbooks. And then we'll see how the same simple techniques apply to everything your child reads, letting him or her pull information out of newspapers, magazines, and so on, almost as fast as the eyes can run down the pages. Here we go!

Signposts in Every Book

1. The Title

Actually, a good title should give you, in a single phrase, the main theme of the book. What it is about, and what it is not about. It is your first concrete information about what you are to learn in the pages that follow. Make sure you understand it before you read on.

What the Title Tells You

The title of this book is *How to Double Your Child's Grades in School.* Here is a deliberately long title, containing two separate pieces of information. First, the subject, which is your child's grades in school. Second, a specific goal—to double those grades.

Starting from this title, and knowing exactly what you should get out of this book, you read on with one purpose—to answer the question *how?*

- *How do I double my child's grades?*

To answer this question, you turn to the next big signpost of the book:

2. The Table of Contents

The Table of Contents takes the grand plan, the ultimate goal you are shooting for, and breaks it down into a step-by-step process. It shows you the steps you have to take, one after another, to attain that goal.

What the Table of Contents Tells You

The Table of Contents is actually a ready-made outline of the book that should be studied carefully before you read one word of its text. By carefully going over the Table of Contents, you immediately gain three things.

1. You gain an overall picture of the skeleton of the book.

2. You see the relationships between each of the various chapters and the main theme of the book.

3. You learn exactly where you will be going when you start to read—to such a degree that you can even set up a time schedule of so many days per chapter to finish the book when you have to.

Table of Contents: The Grand Plan

In this book, the Table of Contents is broken down into six main parts, and then into twenty-six chapters, an epilogue, and the Index.

EXAMPLE

Let's start with the main parts first, and see how they give the overall plan of the book at a glance. Here they are:

1. *The Simple Strategy of Top Grades. (What we are going to do and how we are going to do it.)*

2. *Digging Out the Facts—Reading.*

3. *Expressing the Facts in Writing.*

4. *Mathematics Can Be Fun, If You Do It This Way.*

5. *Mastering Facts—The Art of Remembering and Review.*

6. *How to Breeze Through Tests.*

The Six Parts of This Book

By simply glancing at these six titles, you immediately see that the book is going to concentrate on reading, writing, and mathematics to the extent of devoting full sections to each of them. Then it's going to show your child how to review for tests and make top grades in them.

Thus the general goal of doubling your child's grades, which was promised in the title, has now been broken down into specific, step-by-step goals of improving reading, writing, and mathematics, helping your child over problem areas, and sharpening the ability to take tests.

Now the Table of Contents goes on to show us more concretely how to accomplish each one of these major goals. It does this by listing the chapter headings under each of them. For example, in Part Three of this book, on writing, we find three chapters.

- *Neatness and Legibility—The First Essentials.*   **The Three**
- *Correct Spelling Made Easy—Using the* **Chapters in** *Three-Step System to Improve Your* **Part Three** *Child's Spelling.*
- *Writing Made Easy—How Students Can Write as Easily and Quickly as They Think.*

Now you can see that there are three steps to improve your child's writing. First neatness; then spelling; then the actual construction of sentences and paragraphs.

Again we see the grand plan of the book developing before our eyes. From the overall goal of doubling your child's grades, we have taken one of those steps, which is reading, and learned three ways in which it alone can be improved.

We can do the same thing for each of the other five major parts of the book. Each major part of the book has its own chapter headings underneath it, which show you step by step how you are going to achieve it.

You have now finished reading the title and the Table of Contents. You have spent perhaps five minutes on the book so far. And you already know:

1. What the book is going to do for your child.
2. How it is going to do it, perfectly.

From this point on, you will read simply to answer the questions each one of these chapter headings has raised in your mind. For example, going back to the section on reading again:

How do I improve my child's neatness and legibility?

How do I get my child to spell a word correctly when he or she has misspelled it every time before now?

What are the techniques that allow my child to write easily and quickly?

At this point you could open to the first page of text, and read faster and with much greater understanding than you have ever read before.

But, before you do this, there are two other big signposts you will want to check, to help you get every ounce of information out of that book.

3. The Index

The Index is a storehouse of minor topics of special interest to you. There they are, alphabetically arranged for instant reference.

What the Index Tells You

Glance at the Index of this book. Pick out a topic of special interest to you, or a problem that your child is facing today. For instance, take *fractions.* Look *fractions* up in the Index. Turn to the pages indicated there. *And glance at, do not read,* the treatment given to them.

EXAMPLE

Instantly you can see the concrete, step-by-step methods that make those fractions easy. There's no need to read them word for word now since you'll get to them later this week. And in the proper time and place in the book, they'll mean far more to you.

But now you know fractions are in the Index, and that they're complete. And if you ever have to refer to them after you finish the book, the Index will tell you where they're located at a glance.

And now we turn to the last of our big signposts:

4. The Introduction, Preface, or Foreword

The author gives a personal message, before getting down to the body of the book. In it, you may find:

What the Introduction Tells

- Why the author chose this particular title.
- What compelled the author to write the book.
- A brief, one- or two-paragraph condensation of the book's contents.

- A list of the main sources for the information.
- A list of the reasons why this book should be important to you.
- A brief outline of where you will be heading in the book and what benefits it will give you.

It is the personal note, the personal touch that rounds out your quick survey of the book and gives you insight into the author and the book's purpose, as well as its contents.

The Introduction to this book is divided into three distinct parts, each of which serves a very definite purpose.

EXAMPLE

- Part 1 of the Introduction points out the overwhelming importance of top grades to your child's future and lists nine reasons why they are so vital.
- Part 2 shows you that these door-opening top grades are not that hard to get and, once the right technique is learned, are actually well within the reach of any student of average or better ability.
- Part 3 lists eight specific benefits your child will gain simply by putting the techniques contained in this book to work.

The Introduction to this book, therefore, is an attempt to encourage you and your child with these three facts: that the goal you bought this book to attain is worthwhile, that it is obtainable, and that it will give you the results you wish.

When you have finished this Introduction, you know exactly what goals you are out to get. Then, reading on through the Table of Contents, you realize, step by step, exactly how you are going to get them.

In your one brief survey of this book, or any other, you now know exactly what it is you want to get out of it, and where it is located. You are now ready to read the text itself. To cut through it to the heart of its main ideas, and do it almost as fast as your eyes can move down the page.

Let's now turn to the individual chapters, and see how this same exact method—looking for signposts first—can again mine their information for you at a single glance.

IN SUMMARY ....

No matter how bright your child may be, he or she cannot understand assignments simply by reading them word by word.

Instead, your child must first *pre-read* those assignments—make a quick survey of them *before* reading to uncover their main thoughts.

Your child does this, not only with each chapter assigned, but with each new book that he or she studies.

Your child finds the main ideas of each of these books by checking the four signposts of every book.

1. The Title   **Four Signposts of**
2. The Table of Contents   **Every Book**
3. The Index
4. The Introduction, Preface, or Foreword

By lifting these signposts out of the text and arranging them in order, your child will have at hand an outline of the main thoughts of that entire book.

Your child can then read each individual chapter in order, with perfect understanding of how it ties in to the chapter that has gone before it, the chapter that follows it, and the main theme of the book as a whole.

To the Student: Do It Yourself

- Pre-read assignments and make an outline of an assignment by looking for the four signposts:
  1. The Title
  2. The Table of Contents
  3. The Index
  4. The Introduction, Preface, or Foreword
- This will improve your understanding of the main theme of the book as a whole and will help you to understand it better.

Now let's see how easy it is to pull out the main thoughts of each chapter in the same exact way.

CHAPTER 7

SIGNPOSTS OF EVERY CHAPTER

• • •

What Each Signpost Tells You

In the section above, when we looked at the four big signposts in every book—the Title, the Table of Contents, the Index, and the Introduction—we used this book as our example. And we used *you* as the subject, to show you how these big signposts can help even an intelligent adult get far more information out of any book, in far less time.

The same technique is used by your child the first time he or she opens a new textbook. Using this technique, your child gets a bird's-eye view of the entire course, on the first day. During the rest of the school term, chapter by chapter, your child is merely filling in important details, deepening an understanding of the grand plan discovered in the first survey of a book.

To do this, your child applies to each individual chapter the same quick-survey technique used at the beginning of the book.

To illustrate this technique in action, let's turn now to three fresh examples from typical textbooks students will meet in school.

And let us see exactly what your child should do to them, step by step. How much material he or she has left—and how much was discarded—when your child has finished reducing them to their main thoughts. And how he or she commits that material to memory, for good.

Here are these examples, first reproduced word for word (I suggest you simply glance over them briefly now):

Chapter from a Sixth-Grade English Grammar Book

THE FOUR KINDS OF SENTENCES

A DECLARATIVE SENTENCE makes a statement. It is followed by a period.

EXAMPLE: Poochie is a dog.

An INTERROGATIVE SENTENCE asks something. It is a question, followed by a question mark.

EXAMPLE: Do you have a dog?

To find the subject of an INTERROGATIVE SENTENCE, simply turn it into a declarative sentence.

EXAMPLE: You do have a dog.

An EXCLAMATORY SENTENCE shows surprise or excitement and is followed by an exclamation point.

EXAMPLE: What a thrilling thought!

Sometimes an exclamatory sentence has to be changed to a simple declarative sentence before it is clear what the subject and predicate are.

EXAMPLE:
A. Exclamatory:
    How Dick and John hate each other!
B. The same sentence turned into a declarative sentence:
    Dick and John hate each other, how.

An IMPERATIVE SENTENCE gives a command. It is followed by either a period or an exclamation point.

EXAMPLE: Tell me where you were!

In an imperative sentence, the word you is always understood to be the subject.

EXAMPLE: (You) tell me where you were!

Chapter from a Middle School Text

THE HUMAN BODY

A Living Machine

Human beings are amazing, living machines that come in all sizes, shapes, and colors. Our main features consist of a body covered with skin, as well as our various body parts—a head with eyes, ears, nose and mouth. Two arms, to which our hands are attached, and two legs, to which our feet are attached, all connected to the torso. Our senses—sight, hearing, taste and smell. Our brain and all our other organs. We may look different on the outside, but young or old, tall or short, wide or narrow, we are all very much the same inside. (1)

Vertebrates and Mammals

Humans are vertebrates which means that we have an inner supporting skeleton of bone, including a main backbone. Humans are also mammals. Mammals are warmblooded creatures. Their bodies are covered with hair or fur. Mother mammals feed their babies milk from special glands in their bodies called mammary glands. What makes the human species different from other mammals is our most important organ, the brain. Our brain enables us to think and reason, memorize and remember, decide how to behave and choose what to do and say. (2)

Genes

Genes are a complex set of instructions that tell our bodies how they are supposed to grow and function. Genes also help to determine our appearance. Each human body has anywhere from 100,000 to 200,000 genes. We inherit half our genes from one parent and half from the other. That is why certain characteristics, such as red hair, blue eyes or the ability to wiggle your ears, run in your family. But each one of us has our own physical experiences—from the foods we eat, to the kinds of places where we live. And that makes us unique. (3)

Chemical Structure

The human body is made up of more than 20 different chemical elements. These chemical elements are made up of atoms and they include oxygen, carbon, hydrogen, nitrogen, calcium and phosphorus. Other elements are present in small amounts and are therefore called "trace elements". The human body takes its form from the unique way that all these chemicals combine. For example, oxygen and hydrogen are invisible gases, but when two atoms of hydrogen combine with one atom of oxygen, you get water. And each human body is about two thirds water!

Other elements combine into molecules to form the proteins which make up skin, bones, muscles and blood. The chemical elements in our bodies are constantly being cycled out. Fresh chemicals are supplied by the foods we eat. That is why it is so important to maintain a healthy diet based on a variety of foods.   (4)

Systemic Structure

Our bodies are organized into approximately 12 major systems including the circulatory system, which pumps our blood; the digestive system, which processes food; the muscular system, which produces movement; and the sensory system which detects what happens around the body. The major parts of each body system are called organs. Organs are made of tissues. Tissues are made of cells. Cells are the microscopic building blocks of the human body. The body's largest organs are the skin and the liver. The smallest organs are the touch sensors in our skin, and the lymph nodes that protect us from disease.   (5)

Chapter from a High School Textbook on World History

THE GREEKS: THE BACKGROUND

The ancient Greeks developed the first government that might be called democratic and the first great civilization to take permanent root on the mainland of Europe. Yet the Greek civilization that matured almost twenty-five hundred years ago was by no means purely European in character. The Greeks inhabited the western coast of Asia Minor and the islands dotting the Aegean Sea as well as the European peninsula we call Greece. They also inherited some of the legacy of the older Near Eastern civilizations, probably passed on to them through the Aegean civilization.   (1)

Aegean Civilization

Aegean civilization, which lasted for some two thousand years down to about 1100 B.C., apparently centered on the island of Crete at the southern entrance to the Aegean Sea. Crete had many natural advantages. Its mild climate favored agriculture; the sea gave it some protection against invasion and conquest and at the same time promoted seafaring. Located at the crossroads of the eastern Mediterranean, Crete was close enough to Asia, Africa and Europe for daring seamen to sail their primitive vessels to Egypt and Greece. Its geographical position doubtless made trade and piracy the natural occupations of the islanders.   (2)

When copper and the manufacture of bronze were introduced, probably from Phoenicia or elsewhere in Asia Minor at some time before

3000 B.C., civilization began on Crete. The civilization is termed Minoan, from Minos, a legendary king, and archeologists have divided it into three main chronological periods: (3)

Early Minoan—down to 2300 B.C.
Middle Minoan—2300 to 1600 B.C.
Late Minoan—1600 to 1100 B.C. (4)

Each of these three main periods is subdivided into three segments, from I to III. The greatest flowering of culture on Crete seems to have occurred during the Middle Minoan III and the late Minoan I and II, between 1700 and 1400 B.C. (5)

We must say "seems to have occurred," for our knowledge of ancient Crete is still incomplete. Up to the beginning of the twentieth century it was so sketchy that no methodical approach to its civilization was possible. Then, in 1900, the British archeologist, Sir Arthur Evans, acting on a well-founded hunch, began excavations at Cnossus in central Crete, a few miles inland from the north shore of the island. He struck "pay-dirt" almost at once and started to uncover what was evidently a very large and very ancient palace, which he termed the "palace of Minos." Subsequent diggings by Evans and others disclosed the sites of more than a hundred towns that had existed before 1500 B.C., a goodly amount of pottery, and stretches of paved road. (6)

More recently, hundreds of tablets with Aegean writing have also come to light, both in Crete itself and on the Greek mainland. Although no Minoan equivalent of the Rosetta stone has been found, one scholar announced in 1953 that by using the techniques of cryptography, he had begun the work of deciphering the tablets. This discovery may eventually revolutionize our knowledge of Crete. Meanwhile, we have very little sure information on Minoan politics, though it is conjectured that Crete, like Egypt, had despotic priest-kings who ruled with the aid of a central bureaucracy. (7)

The archeological remains, however, provide convincing evidence that the Minoans were great builders, engineers and artists. The palace at Cnossus was at least two stories high and filled an area equivalent to a city block. A city in miniature, it had running water, a sewage system, and a kind of playground used for dancing, wrestling and other sports. The palace was begun in the Middle Minoan I period and was often repaired and altered, particularly after Middle Minoan II after a destructive earthquake. As a result, the excavated palace is a maze of storerooms, courtyards, corridors, workshops, living quarters, and government offices. Sir Arthur Evans realized that he had very likely discovered the actual building that had inspired the Greek legend of the labyrinth to which the early Greeks were forced to send sacrificial victims. (8)

The skilled craftsmen of Crete apparently copied Egyptian techniques. They did marvelous work, from huge jars, as high as a man, to delicate little cups, no thicker than an eggshell, decorated with birds, flowers, fishes and other natural designs. Painters executed large frescos of kings and warriors on the palace walls. Ivory, gold and jewels were used for the inlaid gaming boards of the kings and for exquisite statuettes, less than a foot high, of the bare-breasted snake-goddess who was apparently one of the chief objects of worship.   (9)

Crete at the height of its power may have controlled an empire including the other Aegean islands and, perhaps, the Aegean shores of Asia Minor and Greece. The recent work on Aegean tablets, however, suggests that Crete itself may have become an outpost of the Greek mainland rather early. The extent of Minoan *political* influence is highly uncertain; there is less doubt about Minoan *cultural* influence, which very likely reached to other parts of the Aegean world.   (10)

A nineteenth-century German, Heinrich Schliemann, undertook excavations at Troy, in northwest Asia Minor, the scene of Homer's *Iliad,* and at Mycenae on the Greek mainland, the home of Agamemnon, the leader of the Greek forces in the Trojan War of Homer's epic. Schliemann loved Homer so deeply that he devoted his life to proving that the Homeric Trojan War was not poetic invention but historical fact. Schliemann's determination resulted in a great archeological romance—early poverty, business success in America, mastery of the Greek language, marriage to a Greek lady (she could recite Homer from memory!), and finally, later in life, discovery of the site of Troy, though it turned out that what he uncovered was a later city built on the ruins of Homeric Troy.   (11)

Thanks to Schliemann and later experts, we now know that by 1400 B.C. Troy and a group of cities centered at Mycenae in Greece had attained a degree of civilization strikingly similar to what had apparently been reached in Crete centuries earlier. Mycenaean pottery, though made of different materials, is similar to Minoan in design and ornamentation. At Mycenae, the kings were buried in large underground tombs, shaped like beehives, which resembled tombs built earlier in Crete. The cities on the mainland, however, built much more elaborate fortifications than did those of Crete.   (12)

By about 1600 B.C., sporadic groups of invaders were filtering down from the north. They appear to have been Greeks, a people who spoke a language probably much like the classic Greek. The first Greeks seemed to have mixed rather peaceably with the existing populations of Greece, the Aegean islands, and Asia Minor, and to have acquired the Aegean culture that flourished at Mycenae and elsewhere. Later Greek invaders were more warlike and destructive. As tribe after tribe pushed south, the old Aegean civilization grew steadily weaker until it finally perished about 1100

B.C. By that time, the Greeks controlled the entire Aegean area, including Crete itself. (13)

The Setting of Greek Civilization

The forces of nature played a large part in shaping Greek civilization. The climate and geography of the Greek homeland have changed little since ancient times. As in the Mediterranean area as a whole, the rains come mainly between September and May. The summers are long, sunny and dry, but because of the sea breezes they are not intolerably hot. People can live outdoors during the greater part of the year, and they can grow olives and other semi-tropical fruit. The sharply indented coastline and the profusion of mountains make a magnificent natural setting. Nature combines such lavish amounts of sunshine and scenery only in California and a few other parts of the world. (14)

Greece, however, has never had the immense fertile acres typical of California. The quality of the soil is poor, and the valleys and plains, squeezed by the mountains, are on a miniature scale. The rivers and streams are too swift and shallow for navigation; they flood in the rainy season, then dwindle to a trickle or dry up altogether. Local springs can supply the minimum needs of the population during the dry season, but they are not adequate for extensive irrigation. (15)

Greece, in short, has never afforded men an easy living, though it has often provided a reasonably pleasant one. The farms and orchards of ancient Greece produced barley and other grains, fruit, wine, honey and little else. Meat was a rarity. (16)

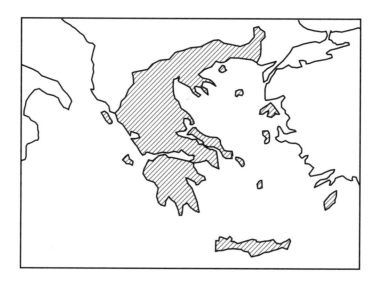

The Greek homeland, however, had one great geographical advantage: its situation encouraged navigation, even by the rather timid. The irregular coasts of the mainland and the islands provided sheltered anchorages; destructive storms seldom occurred during the long summer, the great season of navigation; and the vessels could go for hundreds of miles without ever losing sight of land. Travel in ships propelled by sails or oars or a combination of the two was cheaper, swifter and more comfortable than an up-hill and down-dale journey overland. The Greeks, consequently, built up an active maritime trade.   (17)

The geography of Greece favored political decentralization. In the valleys of the Tigris, the Euphrates and the Nile, the absence of natural barriers to travel had helped the building of large empires. In Greece, on the other hand, the frequent mountains and countless bays and gulfs impeded land communication. The individual valleys and plains, both on the mainland and on the islands, were natural geographic and economic units; they served as separate political units, too.   (18)

The political unit was the polis, or city-state, which included a city and the surrounding countryside. Most of the city-states were exceedingly limited in area; Greece, although a small country, contained many dozens of them. By modern standards, the average Greek city was at best a mere town, and many of its inhabitants were primarily farmers. A strong point, which could be readily defended against attack, was the nucleus of the city. A familiar example is the Acropolis at Athens, with its commanding height and its steep and difficult approaches.   (19)

Chapter from a College Textbook on Business Administration

FIVE ROADS TO COST REDUCTION

Every management is faced with a continuing need to effect cost reduction. Somehow or other we think of these reductions as available principally in the manufacturing process, but this is not the sole area for expense reduction. There are at least five channels through which important savings can be effected. These are: (1)

Raw materials.
The costs of capital equipment.
Manufacturing costs.
Sales expense.
General and administrative overhead expense (including the office). (2)

Although there are some procedures in common which you can use in endeavoring to reduce expenses along these five avenues, for the most part the approaches must be different.   (3)

Road 1: Raw Materials

Raw materials costs vary greatly with industries. Most companies have long since worked out the average percentage of the sales dollar paid for raw materials and supplies. If you can make a comparison of this percentage for your company against other companies in your industry, you may have an excellent starting point. And even where you can't do this, or the comparison is favorable to your company, it nevertheless may pay you to study the ways of lowering the cost of raw materials. Here are the principal devices which companies have used: (4)

1. Development of carefully prepared purchasing specifications, which demand raw material that is good enough for your manufacturing process but not of such high quality that your costs go up out without a compensating increase in the price of your ultimate product.   (5)

2. Inspection of incoming materials to make certain that they meet these specifications.   (6)

3. Tracing back difficulties in the manufacturing process to raw material imperfections.   (7)

4. Modifications of manufacturing processes to eliminate the necessity for certain raw materials and supplies.   (8)

5. Substitution of other kinds of raw materials.   (9)

6. Control over the sources of raw materials either by purchase of supply sources (vertical integration) or by long-term contractual arrangements.   (10)

Road 2: The Costs of Capital Equipment

Piled upon manufacturing costs and material costs must be cost of capital equipment used. Typical of such costs would be depreciation, replacement, maintenance and interest on borrowed capital.   (11)

A great many companies tie up a lot of money in semi-finished or finished inventories. It's useful to make an occasional check as to the amount so tied up and compare it with previous checks.   (12)

Because of inventory pricing policies used by accountants at the close of the year, many a company goes through the year thinking that it has had a profitable operation, only to discover that the inventory pricing has sharply reduced the expected profit.   (13)

In Chapter 4 we shall consider capital financing in more detail, so we shall not make further comment here.   (14)

Road 3: Manufacturing Costs

Manufacturing costs normally consist of labor plus material plus manufacturing overhead.   (15)

Labor opens up a large area for study. It includes proper original selection, adequate training of workers, incentives, supervision, standards and control. It may involve aptitude testing, skill training, time and motion study, work simplification, etc. (16)

Reduction of manufacturing overhead may involve studies of supervision, maintenance and other indirect labor; of inspection and quality control; of fuel, light and power; of fire, safety and insurance protection; of idle equipment charges; of proper utilization of the space available; etc. (17)

Design of new equipment for production involves consideration of manufacturing methods and the capital investment required. (18)

Proper lighting has been responsible for worthwhile increases in productivity and reduction of accidents. Improvements have also resulted from painting of walls and machines, reduction of noise, better ventilation, etc. (19)

Materials handling is usually another fertile field for investigation. The movement and storage of raw materials, work in progress and finished goods can add considerably to the final cost of manufactured goods. (20)

Studies of productive operations may readily include operations research, whereby mathematics is applied to determine the optimum or best manufacturing conditions. Typical would be job lot size to derive the greatest advantage from manufacturing operations; proper inventories of raw materials, partial assemblies, semi-finished products and finished products. (21)

Road 4: Sales Expense

Over the present century there has been a reversal of the relationship of manufacturing cost to marketing costs. At one time manufacturing costs represented more than half the sales price of an article, but these costs have relatively receded so that today, in most companies, the sales costs represent more than half the sales price. Contributing to this increase in sales cost have been such items as warehousing, transportation, advertising, packaging, direct sales costs, and the constant price attrition of competition. Sales overhead, too, has increased through the addition of market research, sales promotion specialists, automatic vending equipment, more sales supervision, etc. (22)

Many sales managers have virtually become sales controllers. Their functions increasingly are those of analysis and control. They need both the accountant's figures as to sales expense and the statistician's figures as to sales analysis. The latter will normally show dollar and quantity sales by salesman, by territory, by customer and product. Wherever the sales manager detects a falling off in some one of these areas, he applies effort to change the condition. (23)

Road 5: General and Administrative Expenses

The fifth avenue of cost reduction consists of analysis of general and administrative expenses. In the normal company these cover such items as salaries of executives and office employees, office expense, interest, property depreciation, taxes, insurance, donations, legal fees, consultants, investigation of possible mergers, economic services and other general business expenses. (24)

Savings through determined effort here can be large indeed. (25)

IN SUMMARY

The five roads to cost reduction are:
1. Raw materials.
2. The costs of capital equipment.
3. Manufacturing costs.
4. Sales expense.
5. General and administrative expenses. (26)

Once possible economies have been uncovered it is necessary to prosecute them vigorously, lest they fail of accomplishment through inertia and resistance to change. (27)

Now Let's Get to Work on Those Chapters. Here's How the Signposts Break Them Down for Your Child

As you could tell at a glance, it's simply not enough for your child to just read these sample chapters, word by word, from start to finish. If your child tries to do this, he or she will confuse detail with main idea, and will remember almost nothing after reading.

What your child needs is a key—a system—that will unlock that mass of words and pull out the main ideas.

This key is PRE-READING: the ability to read chapter signposts at a glance, and use them to pinpoint the main ideas of the chapter, one after the other, and give purpose and direction to reading.

There are eight signposts of every chapter that your child should know as well as his or her own name. Let's review them one by one, and see how they pull the main ideas right out of these chapters *before* your child begins to read the text.

1. Chapter Title

This tells you what the chapter is about, and what it includes and does not include.

In the first chapter, the title "The Four Kinds of Sentences" shows there are a specific number of specific definitions to learn—four. And each of these definitions describes a different kind of sentence. Thus your child knows immediately what to look for—definitions—and how many to find—four.

EXAMPLES

The fourth sample chapter gives the same information in its title. "Five Roads to Cost Reduction" tells your child that he or she must find a specific number of ways to reduce costs—five—and must discover how and in what ways each one works.

The titles of the second and third chapters, "The Human Body" and "The Greeks: The Background," are more vague. They do not tell how many parts are to follow. But they do tell your child what he or she is going to study. Your child must now read on, to the next chapter signposts, to discover what to find out.

2. Section Headings

The section headings break down the overall chapter heading into its main parts. They list the names and number of important subjects to be covered in the chapter. Reading them quickly, without the intervening text, gives the skeleton of the chapter.

The section headings in this sample chapter read as follows:

EXAMPLE from "Five Roads to Cost Reduction"

Road 1: Raw Materials
Road 2: The Costs of Capital Equipment
Road 3: Manufacturing Costs

Road 4: Sales Expense
Road 5: General and Administrative Expenses

Here are the five roads to cost reduction mentioned in the chapter title, laid out for grasping at a glance. Your child now knows the entire structure of the chapter. The only task now is to read the text, and find out *how to* reduce costs in each of these areas.

In this sample chapter, the section headings are a little less specific. They are:

EXAMPLE from "The Human Body"

A Living Machine
Vertebrates and Mammals
Genes
Chemical Structure
Systemic Structure

These section headings provide a guide for your child to follow to determine how these topics relate to the human body.

In this sample chapter, however, the section headings are fewer in number and more vague. They are:

EXAMPLE from "The Greeks"

Aegean Civilization
The Setting of Greek Civilization

These give the two main sources of the background of Greek civilization. But they do not yet give enough information on what to find out about each. Therefore your child must go on to further signposts, which we will describe in a moment.

And in our first sample chapter, there are no section headings at all. So your child checks the next chapter signpost.

3. Paragraph Heads

The paragraph heads tell us the main topic of each paragraph. What the paragraph contains, boiled down into a single phrase.

In this first sample chapter, the author has carefully stated the name of each kind of sentence. Listing them in order, we have:

EXAMPLE from "The Four Kinds of Sentences"

Declarative sentence
Interrogative sentence
Exclamatory sentence
Imperative sentence

Immediately, your child knows the names of the four kinds of sentences to learn in this lesson. Now all he or she has to do is read the text, and find out a definition for each of them.

In the other two chapters, there are no paragraph headings. And so we turn to the next chapter signpost.

4.   Introductory Paragraphs

In introductory paragraphs, the author points out to the student what to look for in the text that follows. He gives an introduction to the chapter, ties it into the chapters that came before it, and often summarizes the main thought or thoughts in the material coming up.

In "The Greeks," the authors begin with this introductory paragraph (for the purposes of this survey, let's break the paragraph apart, point out each of its main thoughts, and state the purpose):   **EXAMPLE**

> The ancient Greeks developed the first government that might be called democratic and the first great civilization to take permanent root on the mainland of Europe.

(This is the introduction to the chapter, pointing out the importance of the Greeks to us all.)

> Yet the Greek civilization that matured almost twenty-five hundred years ago was by no means purely European in character.

(Now the authors lead from the introductory sentence to the non-European background of the Greeks. This is what they are going to discuss in the material that follows.)

> The Greeks inhabited the western coast of Asia Minor and the islands dotting the Aegean Sea as well as the European peninsula we call Greece.

(We are told the first important influence, the geographical setting.)

> They also inherited some of the legacy of the older Near Eastern civilizations, probably passed on to them through the Aegean civilization.

(And now we are told the second vital influence, the Aegean civilization.)

Thus the introductory paragraph confirms the two main divisions in the chapter—the Aegean civilization and the geographical setting—that were revealed earlier by a survey of the section headings. Now your child knows he or she is on the right track. But your child is still looking for further subdivisions. So he or she continues the search to the next chapter signpost.

5. The Summary or Closing Paragraphs

The summary paragraphs are the author's last words on the chapter. They are the author's own outline of the material covered in the chapter before passing on to the next. They are a declaration of what the author deems important out of all the material your child has just read.

Sometimes the author sums up this material in one paragraph, or outlines each idea in a separate phrase, paragraphs it, and may even number it. Sometimes the author rephrases the important points in the form of questions.

In any case, these final words deserve careful study *before* beginning the text.

EXAMPLE Since there are no summary paragraphs in our second and third sample chapters, let's use the one in "Five Roads to Cost Reduction" as our example. It reads:

IN SUMMARY

The five roads to cost reduction are:

1. Raw materials.
2. The costs of capital equipment.

3.   Manufacturing costs.
4.   Sales expense.
5.   General and administrative expenses.

Once possible economies have been uncovered, it is necessary to prosecute them vigorously, less they fail of accomplishment through inertia and resistance to change.

These sentences confirm what your child has already discovered. The five roads to cost reduction are firmly outlined; and, especially on the basis of the last paragraph in the summary, one now only has to read on to discover how to reduce costs in each of these areas.

Your child now turns to the next chapter signpost.

6. The First Sentence of Each Paragraph

As you remember, this pre-reading, this quick survey of an entire chapter before your child begins the text, is essentially a search. A search for the main thoughts of that chapter—for a quick outline of that chapter that tells exactly what he or she is looking for and where to find it.

This search begins with the chapter title, and continues, one by one, with each of the following chapter signposts till your child has uncovered those main ideas—till your child has built an outline.

At this point, after locating the main ideas in the chapter, your child stops the pre-reading and begins the text. The pre-reading is a search for the chapter's main ideas. After finding them, he or she begins to read.

Therefore your child does not check all the chapter signposts in each pre-reading of each chapter. He or she checks only enough signposts to get the main ideas, and then ignores the others.

For example, in "Five Roads to Cost Reduction," your child needed only to read the chapter title, and then the section heads, to find out what the main ideas were—the five roads to cost reduction. Therefore he or she would not even glance at the other chapter signposts, but begin reading the text immediately to find out how to reduce costs in each of these areas.

In the same way, in "The Four Kinds of Sentences," your child needed only to read the chapter title, then check to see that there were no section headings, and then simply pick the main ideas out of the underlined paragraph headings. At that point, he or she had identified the four kinds of sentences, and would immediately begin to read the text to find a definition for each.

However, the second sample chapter, "The Human Body," forces a somewhat deeper survey. Your child needed to read the chapter title and the section headings. But in order to uncover enough of the main ideas to form an outline, your child must go on to read the first sentence of each paragraph as well.

In most cases, especially if the author has done his or her work clearly, these first sentences are called *topic sentences.* They give the main idea of the paragraph and let the remaining sentences fill in the details. So if your child takes the first sentence of each paragraph and strings them together, he or she should have a fairly good outline of the main ideas in the chapter.

First Sentences Are Called Topic Sentences

Unfortunately, this method is not as automatic or as clear-cut as using the first five signposts. Your child has to use more judgment in weeding out paragraphs that don't really contain main ideas.

But in those rare cases when the first five signposts don't do the job, your child must go on with the sixth. Let's see how this method opens up the main ideas in "The Greeks."

Your child has read the chapter title, found only two section headings, found no paragraph heads, discovered that the introductory paragraph merely confirms the two main ideas he or she learned from the section headings, and again found that there was no summary paragraph.

So what has been gained from the first five signposts is this. Your child knows that he or she is to learn about the background of Greek civilization. And he or she knows that there are two sources of this background—the Aegean civilization and the geographical setting of Greece.

What your child still does not know, however, is *what each of these sources contributed to Greek civilization.* He or she has to uncover these contributions—how many there were and what each of them was—before beginning reading with definite, clear-cut goals in mind.

So he or she goes on to identify the first sentence of each paragraph in "The Greeks." (We will give each sentence the number of the paragraph it comes from. And we will leave out the first, introductory sentence, since we have already covered it):

Aegean Civilization

Topic Sentences from "The Greeks"

2. Aegean civilization, which lasted for some two thousand years down to about 1100 B.C., apparently centered on the island of Crete at the southern entrance to the Aegean Sea.
3. When copper and the manufacture of bronze were introduced, probably from Phoenicia or elsewhere in Asia Minor at some time before 3000 B.C., civilization began on Crete.
4. (Unimportant)
5. (Unimportant)
6. (Unimportant)
7. (Unimportant)
8. The archeological remains, however, provide convincing evidence that the Minoans were great builders, engineers and artists.
9. (Unimportant)
10. Crete at the height of its power may have controlled an empire including the other Aegean islands and, perhaps, the Aegean shores of Asia Minor and Greece.
11. (Unimportant)
12. Thanks to Schliemann and later experts, we now know that by 1400 B.C. Troy and a group of cities centered at Mycenae in Greece had attained a degree of civilization strikingly similar to what had apparently been reached in Crete centuries earlier.
13. (Unimportant)

The Setting of Greek Civilization

14. The forces of nature played a large part in shaping Greek civilization.
15. (Unimportant)

16. (Unimportant)
17. The Greek homeland, however, had one great geographical advantage: its situation encouraged navigation, even by the very timid.
18. The geography of Greece favored political decentralization.
19. (Unimportant)

These are the first sentences of each important paragraph in the chapter. Already, in choosing them, the boiling-down process has begun. Already unnecessary words and details have been thrown out. Your child is looking only for main ideas. He or she therefore chooses only those paragraphs that contain those main ideas.

But how does your child know which paragraphs to choose and which to leave out? In a very simple way.

Your child already knows the main theme of the chapter, which was given in the chapter title, "The Greeks: The Background."

Your child already knows the two main sources of that background, Aegean civilization and the geographical setting, which were given in the section headings.

He or she does not know, however, how many divisions each of these two sources has, and what each contributed to Greek civilization. This is the information to look for in the first sentence of each paragraph.

And your child is looking only for big contributions, not details.

Therefore he or she will judge each sentence by these two simple rules:

Two Rules of Every Sentence

1. *They must talk about the main theme of the chapter, and not about some side issue.*

In this case, they must talk about the Aegean contribution to the background of Greek civilization, or about the geographical contribution to that background, and about nothing else.

2. *They must bring in a new main point, and not merely furnish details about a main point brought up by the paragraph before.*

These are the two rules of what to leave in and what to throw out. They are quite simple to follow. Let's see how they eliminate most of the paragraphs in "The Greeks," and leave only the main points. Each comment here has been given the number of the paragraph (and topic sentence) it refers to.

Topic Sentence Information to Keep from "The Greeks"

Mentions Crete as the center of Aegean civilization. Leave it in. **(2)**

Shows high civilization, based on metals, that Crete contributed to Greeks. Leave it in. **(3)**

Just dates of Minoan culture. No contribution to Greeks. Throw it out. **(4)**

More Minoan periods. Out. **(5)**

Says nothing but that our knowledge of Crete is incomplete. No contribution here. Probably a side issue. Throw it out. **(6)**

Another scientific side issue. Out. **(7)**

Now we get to basic contributions from the Minoans—building, engineering, artistry. Leave it in. **(8)**

Details about Minoan art. We already have art in the sentence above. Leave it out. **(9)**

Discusses Minoan seafaring, politics, war—all picked up by Greeks later on. Leave it in. **(10)**

Side issue. Interesting but not important. Throw it out. **(11)**

Identifies other centers of Aegean civilization. Now we know there were two—Crete and Mycenae. And we know that they both made essentially the same contributions. A good find. Leave it in. **(12)**

Talks about invaders, not Aegeans. Not on topic we want. Throw it out. **(13)**

Identifies forces of nature as first great geographical influence of Greeks. Leave it in. **(14)**

Detail under natural forces (soil conditions). Leave it out. **(15)**

Mere comment on effect of natural forces. Covered already by sentence 14 above. Out. **(16)**

New effect of geographical setting—navigable water. Important. Leave it in. **(17)**

A third main effect—political decentralization. Leave it in. **(18)**

A detail about the political centralization mentioned in the paragraph above—the name of the city-state. Not a main point. Throw it out. **(19)**

Now what has your child left, after throwing out the unimportant paragraphs? Let's see.

Taking the title and section headings as they are, and further boiling down the first sentences to a phrase or two each, this is what your child should end up with:

THE GREEKS: THE BACKGROUND

Aegean Civilization

Located at Crete, Troy, and Mycenae. All made the same contributions.
Contributions were in metals, building, engineering, art, politics, seafaring, warfare.

The Setting of Greek Civilization

Greek civilization was shaped by (1) the forces of nature; (2) by the easily navigable waters surrounding Greece; and (3) by the Greek terrain, which made for political decentralization.

With this outline at hand, your child now begins reading the text to make sure he or she understands each of these main points.

However, had your child not been able to get all the main points from the first six chapter signposts, he or she still had two more that might have been able to help. Let's briefly glance at these now:

7. Illustrations

Illustrations, charts, graphs, photographs, etc., are pictorial presentations of the main ideas in each chapter. They boil down great amounts of information, and give them to your child at a single glance. Often they convey information that simply could never be put into words.

The map on page 72 shows the geographical setting of Greece quite vividly. At a glance, your child sees the wonderful advantages Greek mariners had to explore the entire Mediterranean. This confirms the main idea concerning the easily navigable waters surrounding Greece.

EXAMPLE from "The Greeks"

8. Marginal Titles

Marginal titles take the main point of each paragraph and set it in bold type in the margin next to the text of the paragraph. They thus build a walking outline of the chapter for you in the margin. Unfortunately, however, they are not used in modern textbooks to any great extent; and your child must get the same information from the paragraph head mentioned above.

None of our four sample chapters uses marginal titles. However, if "The Greeks" sample chapter did use them, they would look like this:

EXAMPLE

When copper and the manufacture of bronze were introduced, probably from Phoenecia or elsewhere in Asia Minor at some time before 3000 B.C., civilization began on Crete. The civilization is termed Minoan, from Minos, a legendary king, and archeologists have divided it into three main chronological periods . . .   (3)

Beginnings of Minoan Civilization

⟋ IN SUMMARY ....

When reading an individual chapter or lesson in a book, your child uses the same pre-reading, quick-survey technique first used to understand the book as a whole.

Your child uses this quick-survey technique to pull out the main ideas from the chapter before reading it.

Your child finds these main ideas by checking the eight chapter signposts.

1. Chapter Title
2. Section Headings
3. Paragraph Heads
4. Introductory Paragraphs
5. Summary Paragraphs
6. First Sentence of Each Paragraph
7. Illustrations
8. Marginal Titles

The Eight Chapter Signposts

When lifting these chapter signposts out of the text and arranging them in order, your child will have an outline of the main thoughts of that chapter at his or her fingertips.

Your child may then flash-read that chapter—merely skimming over the unimportant details—and concentrating only on definite information on each of these main thoughts.

To the Student: Do It Yourself

- Pull out the main ideas from a chapter or lesson by finding the eight chapter signposts:
  1. Chapter Title
  2. Section Headings
  3. Paragraph Heads
  4. Introductory Paragraphs
  5. Summary Paragraphs
  6. First Sentence of Each Paragraph
  7. Illustrations
  8. Marginal Titles
- You have an outline of the main thoughts of the chapter.
- Now read the chapter to focus on these main thoughts and skim over the unimportant details.

We now turn to a simple trick that will automatically show your child exactly what information to look for on each one of those main points.

CHAPTER

TURNING THOUGHTS INTO QUESTIONS

• • •

How Asking the Right Questions
Can Pinpoint Necessary Information

Now let's list the outlines your child has built by pre-reading the four sample chapters in this book.

In the first sample chapter—the simplest one—here is the outline:

The Four Kinds of Sentences   **EXAMPLE from**
1. Declarative sentence   **"The Four Kinds**
2. Interrogative sentence   **of Sentences"**
3. Exclamatory sentence
4. Imperative sentence

In the second sample chapter, this is the outline your child has worked out:

The Human Body

A. A Living Machine
   1. Human beings are amazing living machines.

B. Vertebrates and Mammals
   1. Humans are vertebrates and also mammals.

C. Genes
   1. A complex set of instructions telling our bodies how to grow and function.

D. Chemical Structure
   1. The human body is made up of more than 20 different chemical elements.

E. Systemic Structure
   1. Our bodies are organized into approximately 12 different systems.

In the third sample chapter, this is the outline your child has worked out:

The Greeks: The Background

A. Aegean Civilization
   1. Located at Crete, Troy, and Mycenae. All made the same contributions.
   2. Contributions were in metals, building, engineering, politics, seafaring, warfare.

B. The Setting of Greek Civilization—Geographical Influences
   1. The forces of nature.
   2. The easily navigable waters surrounding Greece.
   3. The Greek terrain, which made for political decentralization.

And in the fourth sample chapter, the outline emerged like this:

Five Roads to Cost Reduction

1. Raw Materials
2. Capital Equipment
3. Manufacturing Costs
4. Sales Expense
5. General and Administrative Expenses

At this point, your child has the main ideas of each sample chapter at his or her fingertips. But your child's knowledge of the chapter is, of course, still incomplete. *Now your child must read the text itself, to find out what to know about each one of these main points.*

And how does your child tell—again in advance of actually reading the text—exactly what to know about each one of these points?

The answer is simplicity itself. Your child merely:

1. Turns each one of these main points into a question.

And then

2. Reads the text to find out the answers.

It's as easy as that. Now let's see this question-and-answer technique in action.

Six Tiny Keys to Knowledge: Six Basic Questions

Any idea—any word, any phrase, any sentence—can be turned into a question simply by putting in front of it one of these six little words:

Turn any Idea into a Question

- *What?*
- *Why?*
- *Where?*
- *When?*
- *Who?*
- *How?*

The Six Tiny Keys to Knowledge

These are extremely valuable words. You should make your child memorize them from the very first grade on. They have been called, and rightly so, the Six Tiny Keys to Knowledge. Let's see what they can do when we apply them to the main thoughts in each of our sample chapters.

Turning the First Sample Outline into a Series of Questions

First, your child starts with the chapter title. Placing the word *what* in front of it, he or she gets:

EXAMPLE from "The Four Kinds of Sentences"

- *What are the four kinds of sentences?*

This question has already been answered by the section headings in the outline—declarative, interrogative, exclamatory, and imperative. So your child puts the same question to each of these four kinds of sentences, like this:

Keep Asking the Same Question

- *What is the definition of a declarative sentence?*
- *What is the definition of an interrogative sentence?*
- *What is the definition of an exclamatory sentence?*
- *What is the definition of an imperative sentence?*

Your child now knows exactly what information to look for about each one of the main points. He or she now reads to answer these questions, to discover that information, and skims over everything else.

Know Exactly What to Look For

Turning the Second Sample Outline into a Series of Questions

Again, your child starts with the chapter title. Placing the word *what* in front of it, he or she gets:

EXAMPLE from "The Human Body"

- *What is the human body?*

Then he or she goes on to the section headings and by relating them back to the topic, the human body, your child develops the following questions:

Then Go Back to Section Headings

- *How is the human body like a living machine?*
- *Why are humans vertebrates and mammals?*
- *What are genes?*
- *What is the chemical structure of the human body?*
- *What is the systemic structure of the human body?*

Your child now reads the sections to obtain the specific information needed to answer these questions.

Then Go on to the Section

Turning the Third Sample Outline into a Series of Questions

As before, your child starts with the chapter title. Placing the word *what* in front of it, you get:

EXAMPLE from "The Greeks"

- *What are the background sources of Greek civilization?*

This question has already been answered in the two section headings—the Aegean civilization and the geographical setting. So your child questions each one of the section headings in turn, like this:

Then Question the Section Headings

Placing the word *where* in front of the first section heading, your child gets:

- *Where was Aegean civilization located?*

The paragraph headings answer this question—at Crete, Troy, and Mycenae. So your child asks again:

- *What were their contributions to Greek civilization?*

Again your child has the answers—in metals, building, engineering, politics, seafaring, warfare. So he or she asks again:

- *What did the Aegean civilization contribute to the Greek civilization in metals?*
- *What did it contribute in building?*

- *What did it contribute in engineering?*
- *What did it contribute in politics?*
- *What did it contribute in seafaring?*
- *What did it contribute in warfare?*

These are the questions in this section that your child reads on to answer. He or she then turns to the second section, and questions its heading.

- *What were the geographical factors that helped shape Greek civilization?*

Your child has the answers—forces of nature, navigable waters, rough terrain. So he or she questions each one of these factors in turn.

- *How did the forces of nature help shape Greek civilization?*
- *How did navigable waters help shape Greek civilization?*
- *How did the rough terrain help shape Greek civilization?*

Your child now knows exactly what information to look for about each one of the main points. He or she now reads to answer these questions, to discover that information, and skims over everything else.

Turning the Fourth Sample Outline into a Series of Questions

Once again, your child starts with the chapter title. Placing the word *what* in front of it, he or she gets:

EXAMPLE from "The Five Roads to Cost Reduction"

- *What are the five roads to cost reduction?*

The section headings give the answers—raw materials, capital equipment, manufacturing costs, sales expense, and general and administrative expenses. So your child questions each one of these section headings in turn, like this:

- *How can my firm cut raw materials costs?*
- *How can my firm cut capital equipment costs?*

- *How can my firm cut manufacturing costs?*
- *How can my firm cut sales costs?*
- *How can my firm cut general and administrative costs?*

Your child now knows exactly what information to look for about each one of the main points. He or she now reads to answer these questions, to discover this information, and skims over everything else.

Using This Question-and-Answer Technique to Skim Newspapers and Magazines

Your child has now finished pre-reading each chapter and has done this pre-reading in three simple and logical steps. He or she has:

The Three Steps to Pre-Reading

1. Checked the chapter signposts.
2. Used them to pull out the main ideas of the chapter.
3. Turned those main ideas into questions, and will now read to answer them.

This pre-reading, quick survey, question-and-answer technique is one of the most powerful tools of thought your child will ever learn. You should demand that he or she practice it over and over again, until it is automatic.

For example, apply this same technique to newspaper and magazine headlines, to see how it pinpoints the important information at a glance.

First, look at newspaper headlines, with the headlines first, and the questions immediately afterward.

School Board Again Target of Hecklers

- *Why?*

Parents' Group Presses Demand for Principal's Transfer

- *Which principal?*
- *Why has the transfer been demanded?*

- *What exactly does the parents' group want done?*
- *What are the chances of its being done?*
- *What will happen if it is done? If it is not done?*

Highway Blocked by Environmental Study

- *Which highway?*
- *Why is it being blocked?*
- *Who will be affected?*
- *What will happen because of this block?*
- *What are other ways to solve highway problems?*

President Confers on Move in Union Crisis

- *What is the crisis?*
- *How long will it last?*
- *What will be its effects?*
- *What will the government do to meet it?*
- *How soon can they act?*
- *What will happen if they are successful? If they are not?*
- *What will happen next?*

Focus on the Important Issues

You can see immediately what this technique does. It centers your child's attention on the important issues, and prevents being distracted by minor details. It forces him or her to define those main issues, trace their causes and effects, judge how long they'll last, and estimate what will happen next. It pulls the guts out of the article, as fast as your child can run his or her eye down the page.

And this same technique works equally well in magazines, as in this example:

A Drug to Treat Cancer

- *What is it?*
- *Who made the discovery?*
- *Are the discoverer(s) qualified?*
- *Which treatment is required?*

- *How long would it take?*
- *What are its chances of success?*

✔ IN SUMMARY ···

To pre-read a chapter or an assignment, your child follows three steps:

1. Check the chapter signposts.   **Three Steps to**
2. Use them to pull out the main thoughts of   **Pre-Read a**
   the chapter.   **Chapter**
3. Turn those main ideas into questions.

Your child does this by placing the words *what, why, where, when, how,* or *who* in front of the thoughts.

And when your child has turned them into questions in this way, he or she then reads the text to answer those questions, and skims over everything else.

To the Student: Do It Yourself

- Turn the chapter's main thoughts into questions, by placing the words *what, why, where, when, how,* or *who* in front of these thoughts.
- Read each chapter to find the answers.
- Skim over everything except the answers to your questions.

Let us now see how your child slashes through that text, mastering its content, without repetition, in a single flash-reading.

HOW TO POWER-READ

. . .

Mastering an Assignment in Minutes

Your child has now finished this quick survey of the chapter. He or she has pulled out its main thoughts and turned them into questions and is now ready to read the text, word by word, to answer these questions.

Let's see how your child does this, in the shortest possible time, without missing a single vital point.

How to Double Your Child's Reading Rate

Always, of course, our first goal is to improve your child's ability to understanding everything he or she reads. But this search for understanding does *not* conflict with a second vital goal—to speed up your child's reading rate.

Fast readers are good readers. And most children who read slowly do so because of one or two crippling habits they've picked up in the first or second grade. Eliminate those habits and you liberate tremendous new reading speed in your child overnight.

Since your child will be faced with a flood of paperwork in a lifetime, *now* is the time to build in that speed. Here are five simple tricks that will do it for your child automatically:

1. Don't let your child *point out* the words using a finger or a pencil. This slows a reader up. Have your child read *with the eyes only.* This means your child's hands must be folded until turning to the next page.

    Five Simple Tricks to Double Your Child's Reading Rate

2. Keep your child from moving his or her lips or mouth. Lip moving slows reading speed down to speaking speed. If it's difficult for your child to stop lip moving, have him or her bite a pencil while reading till losing the habit.

3. Don't let your child move his or her head from side to side. This tires your child and again slows up reading. *Only the eyes should move. Only eyes need to move.*

4. Teach your child to read aggressively. Actively. Tearing the ideas out of the pages with the techniques we are showing in this book.

5. Teach your child the habit of skimming and then concentrating as described below. Make every reading assignment a search for main thoughts through a forest of the less important words, which he or she skims. Concentrate only on the vital 10 percent.

And then have your child practice. Practice—practice—practice. Till he or she becomes an expert. Till these habits become second nature. Till your child can zip through any written page, anywhere. Like this.

How to Flash-Read Through Unimportant Details

Now, with these speed-reading skills firmly implanted in your child's mind as automatic habits, he or she begins to attack the chapter, word by word.

Your child begins to read as fast as he or she can, reading every word. *But now sifting those words—judging them—accepting them or rejecting them.*

Your child is looking for specific answers to specific questions—the questions he or she constructed in the quick survey before beginning to read.

Look for Specific Answers

These questions should be set firmly in your child's mind:

Put These Questions Firmly into Your Child's Mind

- *What is the definition of a declarative sentence?*
- *How did the forces of nature help shape Greek civilization?*
- *How can my firm cut raw materials costs?*

Every word, every phrase, every sentence that your child's eye flashes over is judged by whether they answer those questions.

Judge Every Word

If they answer the questions, your child stops, concentrates, and underlines, as shown later in this chapter.

If they do not answer the questions, he or she reads on, searching for the answers.

In this way, your child merely skims over 90 percent of the text—the unimportant 90 percent—the excess details, the side issues, the interesting opinions and prejudices that will never be asked for in a test.

Your child reads them all quickly, once. He or she skips none of them, lets them register in

Skip Nothing

his or her brain as they will, lets them fill in the details of the vital points he or she will later concentrate on. Your child makes no deliberate conscious effort to memorize any of them.

But—because at the same time your child is building up a structure of one vital thought in the chapter after another—he or she will find that these skimmed-over details, somehow automatically, stick to these main thoughts.

Stick to the Main Thoughts

Your child will find that he or she remembers far more of this chapter—main thoughts and details both—than were ever remembered before.

The reason for this increase in memory is simple. We remember what we can understand and what we can organize. Trying to memorize nonsense words or jumbled sentences, for example, is almost impossible. And, to your child, a chapter that is not broken down into main thoughts and details is really nothing but a meaningless jumble.

But once your child picks out its main thoughts and puts them in order, he or she has constructed a *memory framework*. From that moment on your child has a logical structure, a set of pigeonholes, for details in his or her memory.

Construct a Memory Framework

Then, even though your child skims over these details and concentrates only on consciously memorizing main thoughts, *the details logically stick to their parent thoughts, and he or she gets them in his or her mind as a sort of no-work bonus.*

So your child has now flash-read 90 percent of the chapter—simply glanced at the details to pick them up—and he or she is *now ready to go to work on main thoughts.*

Here's how your child does it.

The Magic Key to Concentration

As you remember, your child is reading to find specific answers to specific questions. Every sentence is judged on that basis. Does it answer the questions or does it not?

Look for Specific Answers

- *If it does not, your child flash-reads it, and searches on for the answers.*
- If it does, however, your child slows down, concentrates full attention on that sentence, *and picks up a pencil or marker to underline or highlight the answer.*

This deliberate physical act—this aggressive underlining or highlighting of answers in the textbook as they are read—is the Golden Rule that makes your child's concentration automatic. (Of course, students should only write in books if they have their teacher's permission. If it is not possible to underline, you might consider photocopying some text for your child.)

How to Make Your Child's Concentration Automatic

This marking converts routine reading into active, physical thought. It prevents your child's mind from wandering. It makes the dead, lifeless material in the book come to life with the thrill of personal discovery. It forces your child to evaluate, weed out, judge, emphasize. It is the first great step in turning that material into *your child's own personal acquisition* as he or she hammers it out, answer by answer by answer.

Convert Routine Reading into Active, Physical Thought

And it is as easy as ABC. There is only one simple procedure to follow.

Every time your child finds the answer to one of his or her questions, your child simply:

The Three Magic Keys to Concentration

1. Reads it carefully.
2. Makes sure he or she understands it.
3. Underlines or highlights *once* the specific words he or she is going to use to remember it.

That's all there is to it. On an entire page your child may mark only one or two sentences. In a complete lesson, he or she may make only four or five marks in the book.

But these physical marks are your child's own personal milestones along the road to mastery of that lesson. They are the first active step, not only to *locating* the vital thoughts of that chapter, *but to making those thoughts part of your child's mental inventory for as long as he or she wishes to use them.*

Let's see how this process takes place. Let's put it to work on each of our four sample chapters.

How to Power-Read "The Four Kinds of Sentences"

Let's take the first paragraph of the first sample chapter. Here's how it now stands in the textbook:

A declarative sentence makes a statement. It is followed by a period.

Here's how it should look when your child has finished reading it:

A <u>declarative</u> sentence <u>makes a statement.</u> It is followed by a period.

Your child has underlined or highlighted four words and weeded out the rest. He or she now knows the first kind of sentence and its definition. Your child has answered the first question. He or she now goes on to the second, third, and the fourth, till the lesson is finished.

How to Power-Read "The Human Body"

We'll use paragraph 5 as our example in sample chapter two. This is how it reads in the textbook:

> Our bodies are organized into approximately 12 major systems including the circulatory system, which pumps our blood; the digestive system, which processes food; the muscular system, which produces movement; and the sensory system, which detects what happens around the body. The major parts of each body system are called organs. Organs are made of tissues. Tissues are made of cells. Cells are the microscopic building blocks of the human body. The body's largest organs are the skin and the liver. The smallest organs are the touch sensors in our skin, and the lymph nodes that protect us from disease.

The question your child wants to answer is *what is the systemic structure of the human body?* By the time your child has finished power-reading it, the paragraph should look like this:

> Our bodies are organized into <u>approximately 12 major systems including the circulatory</u> system, which pumps our blood; the <u>digestive</u> system, which processes food; the <u>muscular</u> system, which produces movement; and the <u>sensory</u> system, which detects what happens around the body. The major parts of each body system are called organs. Organs are made of tissues. Tissues are made of cells. Cells are the microscopic building blocks of the human body. The body's largest organs are the skin and the liver. The smallest organs are the touch sensors in our skin, and the lymph nodes that protect us from disease.

Your child has underlined or highlighted nine words and weeded out the rest to obtain a succinct answer to the question. And each of the other questions regarding this chapter can be answered in this same way.

How to Power-Read "The Greeks"

In this chapter, let's take paragraph 17 as our example. Here's how it now stands in the textbook:

> The Greek homeland, however, had one great geographical advantage: its situation encouraged navigation, even by the rather timid. The irregular coasts of the mainland and the islands provided sheltered anchorages;

destructive storms seldom occurred during the long summer, the great season of navigation; and the vessels could go for hundreds of miles without ever losing sight of land. Travel in ships propelled by sails or oars or a combination of the two was cheaper, swifter and more comfortable than an up-hill and down-dale journey overland. The Greeks, consequently, built up an active maritime trade.

As you remember, your child's pre-reading survey already established the question to ask in this section. Here is that question:

How did navigable waters help shape Greek civilization?

With that question in mind, here is how this same paragraph should look when your child has finished power-reading it:

The <u>Greek</u> homeland, however, had one great geographical advantage: its situation encouraged <u>navigation,</u> even by the rather timid. The irregular coasts of the mainland and the islands provided sheltered anchorages; destructive storms seldom occurred during the long summer, the great season of navigation; and the vessels could go for hundreds of miles without ever losing sight of land. Travel in ships propelled by sail or oars or a combination of the two was cheaper, swifter and more comfortable than an up-hill and down-dale journey overland. The Greeks, consequently, <u>built up an active maritime trade.</u>

Your child has underlined or highlighted eight words, and weeded out the rest. These eight words answer the question completely— allow him or her to realize that *the navigable waters surrounding Greece enabled the Greeks to build up an active maritime trade.* This is the main thought of the paragraph. The rest is merely detail.

And so your child continues with the reading, using this same technique to weed out 90 percent of the less significant words in the chapter: to concentrate only on the answers to main-thought questions, thereby building up, answer by answer, the complete, easily remembered Main-Thought Outline of this lesson, which we will examine in the next chapter.

How to Power-Read "Five Roads to Cost Reduction"

As a contrast, let's take paragraph 24 of this sample chapter. Here's how it stands in the textbook:

The fifth avenue of cost reduction consists of analysis of general and administrative expenses. In the normal company these cover such items as salaries of executives and office employees, office expenses, interest, property depreciation, taxes, insurance, donations, legal fees, consultants, investigations of possible mergers, economic services and other general business expenses.

As you remember, the question we were using here was:

How can my firm cut general and administrative costs?

With that question in mind, here is how this same paragraph looks when your child has finished it:

The fifth avenue of cost reduction consists of analysis of <u>general and administrative expenses.</u> In the normal company these cover such items as <u>salaries</u> of executives and office employees, <u>office expenses, interest,</u> property <u>depreciation, taxes, insurance, donations, legal fees, consultants, investigations</u> of possible mergers, economic <u>services</u> and <u>other</u> general business expenses.

Here the answer to the question gives eleven or more ways to cut costs in this area, and all are underlined or highlighted. Later, when building the Main-Thought Outline, your child will combine several of them so they can be more easily memorized.

At the present point, however, your child continues to read on until finishing the chapter, answering each of his or her questions and thoroughly understanding each of its main points.

✍ IN SUMMARY ....

Once your child has made a pre-reading survey, with its questions to be answered, the actual reading of the lesson becomes markedly fast and easy.

During this reading, your child will skim over about 90 percent of the text, searching only for the answers to the main-thought questions, and letting their details stick to his or her memory automatically.

And when your child finds a main-thought answer, he or she actively underlines or highlights it, marking each word to use later for remembering the main points.

In this way, your child actively builds up a series of main-thought answers, *which he or she will now use to build a Main-Thought Outline in a notebook for recalling as often as he or she wishes.*

To the Student: Do It Yourself

- Read over your chapter to search for the answers to your main-thought questions.
- When you find your main-thought answers, underline or highlight them.
- You will now use these main-thought answers to build a Main-Thought Outline in your notebook to help you remember your answers.

It is to this last step of rewriting and remembering that we now turn.

HOW TO
TAKE NOTES

• • •

Remembering What You Read
and Putting It to Use

Your child is now ready for the payoff, the moment when he or she masters the meaning of the chapter and owns it.

What has your child done so far? All this:

1. Picked out the main thoughts of the chapter.
2. Turned them into questions.
3. Weeded out material that did not answer those questions, and which he or she will never have to look at again.
4. Located the answers to those questions—the vital information that composes the backbone of that book.
5. Marked that vital information separate from the rest of the chapter.

Your child now has everything needed to know about every main thought in that chapter right at his or her fingertips. *Now your child has to fit them together.*

Now your child rewrites the chapter in his or her own personal language, making fifty words do the work of five thousand.

Your Child's Notebook: Where to Re-create the Backbone Meaning of Each Chapter, Each Book, Each Course

In addition to his or her own mind, there are only three basic tools to open up the vast world of knowledge to your child's grasp:

- Textbook
- Pencil
- Notebook

In fact, your child's grades in school may very well depend on this ability to transfer knowledge from one of these books to the other.

What exactly *is* this notebook? What should it contain? How should it be arranged? How exactly does your child use it to get the maximum benefit from reading?

Let's look at each of the points in turn.

Your child's notebook is the actual storehouse of everything learned, from every course, during an entire school semester.

That notebook should be large and loose-leafed. It should also have a durable hard cover. It should have plastic, colored separators for each course. It should have your child's name, address, and telephone number written in ink inside the front cover, because it is much too valuable to lose.

Your child should carry this notebook every day, to every class. When he or she sits down at the study table at home at night, it should be the first book to be opened. It is a portable organizer. It sets up his or her entire study schedule in this way:

Each course in the notebook must be set off by a plastic colored separator. The first page following that separator is the assignment page for that course. On that page, each assignment for each day is copied down exactly as it is given by your child's teacher, like this:

April 3

Chapter 2: "Five Roads to Cost Reduction," pages 73 to 76. Answer questions 2 to 8 at end of chapter, to hand in tomorrow.

Each day's assignments are written in this way on the assignment page, one after another. As they are completed, they are checked off with a red pencil. But they are kept in the notebook, to serve as part of the flash review your child will make before he or she takes any test.

Writing Up Each Day's Lesson in the Notebook

After the assignment page for each course, come the Main-Thought Outline pages to write up, day after day.

These pages are not haphazard in any way. They are not written in the classroom, not written while your child is actually reading the text. There is no room on them for illegible scrawls, written daydreaming, or doodles of any kind.

They are carefully and precisely prepared, in this way:

1. When your child has finished reading the chapter and underlined or highlighted the answers to the main-thought questions that were previously prepared, he or she then closes the book. **How to Write Up the Lesson**
2. Your child is now ready to put this knowledge of the backbone of that chapter to its first test. To do this, he or she takes a blank sheet of paper—not in the notebook—and from memory writes down each of the main thoughts of that chapter and the information learned about them.
3. Your child will forget some of these points. He or she will write down some of them out of order. Your child will find that he or she still doesn't clearly understand some of the information about them. None of this is important. What is important is the fact that your child has just made a first recitation, taken the first self-test on that chapter.
4. Your child now goes back to the text and checks and corrects the outline. He or she

writes the corrections directly onto that rough outline.

5.   When your child has finished it, by boiling down and correctly arranging it to his or her own satisfaction, your child then turns that paper over. He or she opens the notebook. And writes that outline—again from memory—on one page of that notebook.

6.   What your child is doing is becoming free, step by step, from the crutch of that textbook. He or she is transferring knowledge out of that textbook into memory, and then into his or her notebook for instant reference. And each step of the way, he or she is condensing that knowledge, memorizing and rememorizing it, understanding it more deeply and clearly with each word that is written.

7.   When your child has finished writing the outline in the notebook, he or she checks it again. If there are one or two errors or omissions, your child writes them in. If there are too many, he or she rewrites the entire page. Your child writes on only one side of the paper, however, in order to use the other side later to double the profit he or she gets out of every hour of review.

And then, when your child has the outline in the notebook finished to his or her satisfaction, he or she closes both books and is finished for the night. Your child has learned this chapter. Your child has the backbone of that chapter stored in his or her memory and notebook, ready to go to work at an instant's notice.

And your child can show it to you every night in your five-minute Achievement Check. Let's see what these finished outlines should look like, for each one of our four sample chapters, when your child proudly displays them in his or her notebook.

The Finished Outline for "The Four Kinds of Sentences"

The Four Kinds of Sentences
1. Declarative—makes a statement.
2. Interrogative—asks something.
3. Exclamatory—shows surprise or excitement.
4. Imperative—gives a command.

The Finished Outline for "The Human Body"

The Human Body
1. An Amazing Living Machine:
   a. Main features consist of the body; the senses; and the organs.

2. Vertebrates and Mammals:
   a. Vertebrates because of inner supporting skeleton, including backbone.
   b. Mammals because we are warmblooded, covered with hair and can feed our children using mammary glands.
   c. The brain differentiates humans from other animals.

3. Genes:
   a. Complex instructions that tell our bodies how to function.
   b. Each body has 100,000 to 200,000 genes.
   c. Inherit half our genes from one parent and half from the other.
   d. Physical experiences make us unique.

4. Chemical Structure:
   a. Comprised of more than 20 chemical elements including oxygen, carbon, hydrogen, nitrogen, calcium, and phosphorus.
   b. Body takes its form from the way chemicals combine.
   c. Elements combine into molecules to form proteins that make up skin, bones, muscles, and blood.
   d. Fresh chemicals to nourish our bodies supplied by food.

5. Systemic Structure:
   a. Bodies are organized into approximately 12 major systems including circulatory; digestive; muscular; and sensory.

    b. Major parts of each body system are called organs.
    c. Largest organs are the skin and the liver.
    d. Smallest organs are touch sensors and lymph nodes.

The Finished Outline for "The Greeks"

The Greeks: The Background

1. Aegean Civilization. Centered at Crete, Troy, Mycenae. Contributions were:
   a. Copper and bronze basis for high civilization.
   b. Advanced engineering techniques produced fortifications and palaces.
   c. Rules by kings.
   d. Empire building through trade and warfare by sea.

2. Geographical Influences:
   a. Poor soil and climate forced Greeks to seek their fortunes overseas.
   b. Easy navigability made sea transportation easier and more profitable than land.
   c. Rough terrain encouraged individual city-states.

The Finished Outline for "Five Roads to Cost Reduction"

Five Roads to Cost Reduction

1. Cut raw materials costs by:
   a. Precise purchasing specifications.
   b. Inspection of incoming materials.
   c. Elimination of manufacturing difficulties due to raw materials.
   d. Substitution or elimination of unnecessary materials.
   e. Financial control of sources.

2. Cut capital equipment costs by:
   a. Reducing costs of depreciation, replacement, maintenance, and interest.
   b. Holding down inventories.
   c. Sharpening accounting procedures.

3. Cut manufacturing costs by:
   a. Better labor management.

   b. Analysis of indirect costs.
   c. Design of new equipment.
   d. Better working conditions.
   e. Improved materials handling.
   f. Operations research.

4. Cut sales costs by cutting costs of:
   a. Warehousing.
   b. Transportation.
   c. Advertising.
   d. Packaging.
   e. Direct sales costs.
   f. New specialist costs.

5. Cut general and administrative costs:
   a. Administrative salaries.
   b. Office expense.
   c. Interest.
   d. Insurance.
   e. Donations.
   f. Legal fees.
   g. Consultants.

Five Tips on Improving Your Child's Outlines

1. Simplify. Keep compressing, boiling down, **Tip One:** making the outline shorter and shorter. **Simplify** Use phrases instead of sentences. Eliminate unnecessary words and details. Blend subordinate sentences into others by boiling them down into one or two words. Keep cutting till each idea stands sharp and clear in a few easy-to-remember words.

2. Fit the ideas together properly. Make sure **Tip Two:** one leads into the other in the right order. **Fit Ideas** Then, when your child thinks of the first **Together** idea, the second automatically pops into his or her mind.

3. What are the kinds of order your child can use to make one idea fit in with another? Here are a few: **Tip Three: Order**

A. Parts of Something. **EXAMPLE**
   Kinds of birds:
   1. Sparrow
   2. Robin
   3. Bluebird, etc.

B. Time Order. **EXAMPLE**
   Battles of World War II:
   1. Poland
   2. Holland
   3. France
   4. Britain, etc.

C. Step-by-Step Sequence. **EXAMPLE**
   How to Build a Model Airplane:
   1. Check each part and arrange in order.
   2. Read instructions carefully.
   3. Cut out all parts, etc.

D. Causes of Something. **EXAMPLE**
   Causes of 1929 Depression:
   1. Watered stock
   2. Insufficient government control
   3. Speculation by banks, etc.

E. Effects of Something. **EXAMPLE**
   Results of 1929 Depression
   1. Vast unemployment
   2. Business bankruptcies
   3. Loss of 1932 election, etc.

F. Arrangement by Space. **EXAMPLE**
   States on the Eastern Seaboard:
   1. Maine
   2. New Hampshire
   3. Massachusetts
   4. Rhode Island, etc.

These are only a few samples. Have your child look for other kinds, and keep a list of them at the back of his or her notebook.

4. Use numbers. They are a great help, both in understanding a lesson and remembering it for future use. For example, once your child knows that there are *five* roads to cost reduction, he or she realizes the need to reproduce all five of them on any future test. If your child had not numbered them, however, he or she may have thought there were only four, and left one out because of not stopping to search for it.

Tip Four: Use Numbers

5. Indent. And then indent again. Physical indentations show instantly the difference between the theme of the entire chapter and its sub-thoughts. And if these sub-ideas have any further divisions, again indentations show their relation at a glance. Notes should be neat and precise, with plenty of white space around each point, so your child can see exactly where it stands in relation to the chapter as a whole when he or she reviews it.

Tip Five: Indent

How Notes Should Be Used

When your child finishes writing up these notes each night, he or she has accomplished not one but two vital tasks. He or she has:

1. Read and understood the chapter assigned—and understood it more completely than ever dreamed before.
2. Stored away the backbone meaning of that chapter, *so that he or she can now thoroughly review it for a test by reading as few as fifty words, instead of as many as five thousand.*

Your child has two enormous advantages over others who do

not use this technique. And he or she begins putting those advantages to use immediately.

Your child's first review takes place right after finishing those notes, in your five-minute Achievement Check that same evening. Here you discover exactly how much your child gained from the day's reading. Here he or she accounts to you now—passing inspection—even before beginning to put this new knowledge to work in class.

The procedure is simple. You read the notes, then ask questions about any point that seems vague or unclear to you. Then you ask your child one or two questions concerning the contents of these notes.

For example, if a point doesn't seem clear to you, ask:

> *"I don't understand how precise purchasing specifications can cut raw materials cost. Would you mind explaining that to me?"*

Or, as an example of a general-review question on the contents of the third sample chapter, ask her or him:

> *"How about giving me those three geographical influences again?"*

Your child should be able to answer each of these questions instantly from memory, without referring back to his or her notes. Soon your child will look forward to these check periods with tremendous anticipation. And you, on your part, must be sure to show the enthusiasm and pride you feel.

When you are through with the individual chapter notes each evening, then test your child's overall mastery of the course by asking these questions, which force him or her to tie in the daily reading with everything learned before:

> *"Why do you think the author placed this chapter where it is in the book?"*
> *"How does it tie in with the chapter you read yesterday?"*
> *"What did you have to know in yesterday's chapter before you could understand the material you read today?"*

These questions force your child to think. To tie in. To relate forward and backward. And to become accustomed to expressing thoughts in his or her own words.

When you are through with that Achievement Check each night, your child knows that he or she has mastered that material. And your child is confident that he or she can talk sense about it to anyone.

The Next Morning

And the next morning, on the way to class, your child takes one more brief look at these notes. Riding or walking to school, walking through the halls, with the notebook closed, he or she runs through these three magic questions:

- *In one sentence, what did I learn from last night's chapter?* (That the five roads to cost reduction are reducing raw materials costs, manufacturing costs, capital equipment costs, sales costs, and general and administrative costs.)
- *How does this tie in with the chapter before?* (It's a second way of increasing profits, right after improved management.)
- *Which questions will I be asked on it in next week's test?* (To list several ways of reducing costs in each one of these areas. And he or she runs through them.)

Using this planned technique, in half the time that it would have taken to read that chapter before, your child is now ready to go into that classroom and make his or her classmates' eyes pop open in amazement.

✔ IN SUMMARY ....

There is an easy, simple, organized way to master the contents of any assignment. It consists of the following three steps:

The Three Magic Keys to Expert Reading

1. Pre-read the assignment, to pick out its main thoughts and turn them into questions.

2. Power-read the assignment, to weed out unnecessary details and concentrate on the answers to these questions.

3. Translate the assignment into a Main-Thought Outline that expresses these answers in as few words as possible, and that is stored for instant review in your notebook.

These are the three Magic Keys to Expert Reading. You should have your child practice them again and again and again, until they become second nature. They will pay dividends for the rest of his or her life.

To The Student: Do It Yourself

Prepare to master the content of any assignment—using the *Three Magic Keys to Expert Reading:*

- Pre-read your text for main thoughts to turn them into questions by placing *what, why, where, when, how,* or *who* in front of the thoughts.
- Power-read the assignment by finding answers to your questions and skimming over unnecessary details.
- Create a Main-Thought Outline from your answers, which have as few words as possible, to practice again and again until you can remember them in an instant.

THE ART OF LISTENING

• • •

Right Down to Reading the Speaker's Thoughts

In addition to reading, your child gains the information needed in school by listening.

In fact, in later life, when going into the business and social worlds, his or her ability to listen well will be even more important than the ability to read well. Most adults gain about 80 percent of all new facts through their ears, not their eyes.

Therefore, hearing everything that is said, and missing nothing, is an indispensable art. *But it is an art. It is not a natural gift. You must teach it. Just as your child must learn how to read, so he or she must learn how to listen in this simple but tremendously powerful way:*

How to Develop Your Child's Listening Power from the Very First Grade

When do you start to develop this ability to listen in your child? The very first moment he or she can understand a fairy tale or story, and answer questions about it. It may be as early as the age of four or five; it certainly should be no later than enrollment in the first grade.

Start this way. Some night, at the dinner table if you have a four- or five- or six-year-old, make up a new game. Tell your child that you're going to read a list of objects—toys, games, the names of his or her friends, what have you. Then ask your child to name back that list in the order in which you gave it. It's as simple as that.

Start with a list of ten objects. See how many your child can name, and how much he or she can improve. Award prizes. At first your child will remember two or three. Then four or five. Then all ten—perfectly.

As your child grows older, make the game harder. Tell a story, and ask him or her to repeat the important facts. Read a newspaper article and then ask questions about it. Try to stick with specific names and figures. Watch your child repeat them back to you, number by number.

You'll be astounded at how much your child can retain. And you've taught the first secret of good listening—strengthening ear-channel memory—learning to remember everything important that one hears.

Now your child is ready for the second step.

How to Concentrate on the Speaker's Thoughts, and Never Be Distracted

Once your child has strengthened his or her listening memory, to hold entire thoughts and sentences in mind after hearing them only once, then he or she is ready to fit them together into meaningful patterns as the speaker talks. There is a definite technique to re-creating the core of a lecture—any lecture—to never forget it. Here's how:

Learning to listen well—to hear everything of real importance that's being said—is primarily a matter of being able to maintain attention, of pacing oneself to follow the speaker's thoughts, and not letting the mind wander off. Because of this fact, the power of complete attention has been called the mark of an educated person.

Why is it difficult to maintain this attention? Because the

human brain thinks about four times as fast as the human tongue can speak. And the huge gap between the speed of the mind and the words being heard provides time for all sorts of distracting personal thoughts.

How does your child keep these distracting thoughts from leading him or her astray? *By forcing him or herself to keep pace with the speaker in these three ways, every time his or her mind is about to wander:*

1. *By summarizing what the speaker has already said, and building it into a Main-Thought Outline.* Here your child asks questions like these:

   Three Ways to Keep the Mind from Wandering

   - How can I sum up these statements in a single phrase?
   - How do they tie in with the speaker's last point?

2. *By anticipating the speaker's next point, with questions like these:*
   - What is the speaker getting at here?
   - Where will the speaker go now?
   - What examples must the speaker give to prove this point?

3. *By listening "between the lines" for points that are not put into words, with questions like these:*
   - What is the speaker implying here?
   - Why does the speaker stick to this one point, and not go on to the other we were discussing last week?
   - Is the speaker hinting at more than he or she is willing to say right out?

And so on, with other questions that will come to your child's mind while seeking the inner meaning of the speaker's words.

All these questions have one vital trait in common: *They turn listening from a passive to an active occupation.* They stop drifting.

They force your child to *think* step by step with the speaker. To keep his or her mind constantly focused on that speaker's thoughts, both expressed and unexpressed. And to pull the core meaning out of that lecture as it develops.

And then, as your child does in reading night after night, he or she stores that core meaning on paper to have it for good.

How to Take Lecture Notes

Your child now has two powerful tools to capture the inner meaning of any spoken statement, lecture, or conversation he or she may hear.

Your child has developed a strong listening memory, to hold entire thoughts and sentences after hearing them only once.

And your child has the ability to keep his or her attention focused on the speaker's thoughts, both expressed and unexpressed, for as long as necessary to pull out the inner meaning of those thoughts as it develops in front of him or her.

Your child now makes these two gifts even more effective by learning how to re-create the backbone meaning of that lecture in his or her own notebook, for instant reference whenever it is needed.

Because a word is spoken once and then is lost forever, lecture notes are prepared differently from reading notes. Though the end result is the same, the technique of capturing the main thoughts must work far faster in the lecture hall than in the reading room.

Here is that technique, step by step.

Sixteen Steps to Perfect Lecture Notes

1. The more your child knows about the material covered by a lecture, the more he or she will get out of that lecture. Therefore your child should always read the material in the textbook before it's covered in the lecture. Then your child can use at least **Read the Assigned Reading Before Class**

part of the lecture as a review, rather than a new learning experience.

2. What your child is looking for in such a lecture is *enrichment*. This is the material that the teacher includes in the lecture that is *not* in the textbook, and that can never be picked up by mere textbook reading alone. This bonus information should form the core of the lecture, and should be what your child brings home in his or her notebook.

    Enrichment: The Bonus Information

3. The lecture pages in your child's notebook should be separate from the reading pages. To begin with, of course, your child will take lecture notes on a piece of scrap paper, where he or she can jot down ideas as they seem important, and cross them out or rearrange them as corrections are necessary. Only after the lecture is over will your child write them up in finished form and put them into the notebook, as we explain below.

    Write Up Final Notes After the Lecture

4. These lecture notes begin the moment your child walks into the room. Your child has already reviewed the textbook material that he or she believes will be covered in the lecture. Prepared to listen, your child takes a seat as far forward in the room as possible, places his or her book and notebook on the floor, leaving on the desk only a piece of scrap paper and pen or pencil.

    Be Prepared to Listen

5. Your child writes at the top of that paper the date, the name of the lecturer if it is different from his or her regular teacher, and

    Identify Time, Date and Lecturer

the subject of the lecture as soon as it is announced.

6. Your child's first goal is to discover the central theme, the main point, the speaker's goal in giving the lecture. He or she finds this out in one of several ways:

Discover the Central Theme

- It may be contained in the lecture title. A lecture on "Five Roads to Cost Reduction," for example, would give the theme immediately.

- If the title is vague, however, then your child must look elsewhere. Perhaps the lecturer distributes notes on photocopied sheets before the lecture. These should be carefully read and the main thoughts underlined or highlighted. If the central theme is given on the sheet, it should be transferred to notepaper immediately.

- If there are no printed notes, then your child must listen carefully to the lecturer's opening remarks. He or she should, of course, disregard introductory acknowledgments, anecdotes, jokes, and so on, and concentrate on picking up such *signal phrases* as the following:

  "I wish to discuss today the problem of—"
  "The theme of my lecture today will be—"
  "Have you ever thought of the extreme
      importance of to this country of—"

Somewhere in these opening remarks, the main theme will emerge. As soon as your child has it, it should be boiled down in his or her mind to one or two phrases, and written at the top of your child's paper. There it will control the development of the outline— to tell exactly what to look for in the rest of the lecture.

How to Recognize the Speaker's Main Points

7. Once your child knows the main theme of the lecture, the next goal is obvious. He or she must chart the development of that central theme through one vital thought after another. Your child is now building an outline from the speaker's words—listening for main thoughts and writing each of them down in order.

   Chart the Development of the Central Theme

8. To do this your child listens 90 percent of the time and writes the other ten. Note-taking is not stenography. It is never merely writing down the exact words the lecturer uses, even if that were possible. Note-taking is condensation. Judgment. Weeding out the unimportant. Boiling down the central thoughts, as they occur, to a few capsule words or phrases, and then fitting them into their place in a growing outline.

   Note-Taking Is Condensation

9. How does your child recognize these main thoughts? In two ways. First because they are *big ideas* pertaining to the central theme of the lecture. (For example, in a lecture on "Five Roads to Cost Reduction," once your child hears the speaker say, *"Now, the first road to cost reduction is, of course, to cut raw materials costs,"* your child knows that he or she has the first main thought.)

   Recognize the Big Ideas

10. Next, your child recognizes the lecture's main thoughts by the *signal words* the speaker uses to introduce them. These signal words are much like the chapter signposts that guided your child to the

    Recognize the Signal Words

meanings in textbook reading. They are verbal signals that flag your child's attention, that warn something really important will follow them. Let's look at a few of them right now.

Any number is a direct giveaway that the speaker is going to list the main points for the audience. The speaker may even give the audience advance notice of how many main points he or she is going to have, in this way:

"Now, the geographical setting of ancient Greece had three main influences upon Greek civilization."

At that point your child marks in rough notes:

Influences of geographical setting:

1. _____

2. _____

3. _____

Your child now knows that there are three geographical influences, and has a space for each of the three as they come up in the lecture. He or she now has a built-in *main-thought trap* in the notes, and listens without writing until the speaker signals again, by saying: *"The first geographical influence."*

Then your child writes it down, and waits for the second and the third.

These number signals are the most clear-cut clues the speaker will give your child to the number and arrangement of the main thoughts. But there are others almost as useful. Here are some of them, and what they tell your child:

- *Next, then, further, besides, moreover, but, in addition:* another important fact is coming.
- *Then, soon, meanwhile, later, at last, finally:* another important event is taking place in the speaker's time sequence.
- *For example, especially, in particular:* the speaker is going to illustrate a main point by a specific case.

- *On the other hand, yet, still, however, on the contrary, but, nevertheless:* a new main point is going to be introduced to contrast with the main point that has just been covered.
- *In conclusion, to sum up, finally, hence, so, thus, as a result:* the lecture is coming to a conclusion (at this point your child should watch for a summing up that will give the chance to check and see whether he or she has all the main points in their right order).

And, finally, here are some other signal words to watch for, because they may point up a main thought that follows them: *all things considered, above all, for this reason, to this end, likewise, and so.*

How the Lecturer Gives Away the Questions Your Child Is Going to Be Asked

11. In addition to these automatic signal words that point out the main thoughts of the lecture, the speaker many times will deliberately pause, then tell the class that such and such a point is going to be asked for in a future test. He or she may use any one of the following forms to announce this:

Identify the Test Questions

- *"It is important to note—"*
- *"Be sure to know—"*
- *"Pay special attention to—"*

Or he or she may come right out and say it:

- *"You'll be asked to—"*
- *"This will be a test question—"*

Once your child hears these clues, he or she sets this point off from the rest of the lecture in this way. Your child marks a large TQ (for Test Question) beside it. Then, in the review later on, your child can give it special attention.

How to Finish the Notes so They Contain Everything Your Child Needs

12. Now, what has your child done so far during this lecture? He or she has:

    Check to See Notes Are Complete

    - Written down the central theme at the top of his paper.
    - Jotted down the main headings either as they were outlined at the beginning of the lecture or as they emerged during its development.
    - Left plenty of room after each of these headings to serve as main-thought traps to pick up their vital sub-points.
    - Filtered out these sub-points by careful, active listening, and by following the clues of the speaker's signal words.

13. Therefore, at the end of the lecture, your child should have the main-thought backbone of that lecture completely down on his or her rough sheet of paper. *Now the job is to rewrite those notes into finished form as soon as possible.*

    Prepare to Rewrite Notes

14. If your child has the time, he or she stays in the lecture hall after the other students have left and rewrites them there. Or in the next classroom, before the class begins, he or she rewrites them there. In any case, your child uses the first available five minutes to fix those notes firmly in his or her notebook and mind.

    Make Time to Rewrite Notes

15. Your child rewrites them in this way. He or she rereads everything put down on that rough sheet of paper, making sure to understand each point and its relation to

    How to Rewrite Notes

every other point in the lecture. Then, if necessary, he or she puts them in the correct and final order. Your child weeds out, numbers, underscores, and organizes until these notes are written as clearly and completely as his or her reading notes every night.

16. This is the first self-recitation of the material in this lecture. When your child has finished it, and fitted it into place behind the other lecture notes, that lecture is his or her own. Your child is now ready to relate it to reading notes on the same material, and put it to use whenever needed for class recitation or a test.

Save Notes for Future Use

Two Other Vital Classroom Techniques

At one time or another during a lecture, your child, no matter how bright, will have a moment of just not understanding one of the speaker's statements, or will have a thought which would modify that statement.

Therefore your child must get into the habit of asking questions, of speaking up in the classroom as well as at home.

If the teacher allows questions during the lecture, your child should ask a brief, polite, to-the-point question immediately. This question should have one purpose: to clear up the point that is vague in his or her mind. Once it is cleared up, your child should write the point and its answer in the rough notes, and check it later to make sure he or she has understood it. As we shall discuss later, any misunderstanding is a golden opportunity for learning.

If the teacher does not permit questions during the lecture, then your child should speak to him or her after class. In any case, your child should never leave the classroom with the question unanswered.

At the same time, if sample problems are done by the teacher during the lecture, or as part of a homework assignment, your child should copy them, word by word, right into his or her notebook.

This is essential—especially in mathematics classes—for these two reasons:

First, because it trains your child away from attempting short-cut methods, where he or she may leave out vital steps and get hopelessly lost. And it eliminates the necessity for your child to copy answers rather than mastering the methods that produce them.

Two Reasons to Copy Sample Problems

(In later life, there will be no pat answers to copy. Then only methods will be of any use. And, if your child is going to compete, he or she had better know them.)

And secondly, this step-by-step copying of sample problems is one more way of assuring attentiveness. Again, the best way by far to learn is actively, with a pencil in your hand.

IN SUMMARY ....

Power-listening can be developed as effectively as power-reading, simply by learning a few easy techniques. These are:

Strengthening your child's listening memory, so he or she can retain whole phrases, thoughts, and sentences after hearing them only once.

Teaching your child to maintain full concentrated attention on the speaker's words, so that no important thought, expressed or unexpressed, can escape him or her.

And showing your child how to boil a lecture down into its vital thoughts, each in its proper order, to store the backbone meaning of that lecture in his or her mind and notebook for instant reference whenever needed.

To the Student: Do It Yourself

- Strengthen your listening memory to hold entire thoughts and sentences in your mind.
- Remember whole phrases, thoughts, and sentences after hearing them only once by learning to listen well.
- Summarize what the speaker has already said, and build it into a Main-Thought Outline. Ask yourself these questions:

  1. How can I sum up these statements in a single phrase?
  2. How do they tie in with the speaker's last point?

- Learn to figure out the speaker's next point by asking:

  1. What is the speaker getting at here?
  2. Where will the speaker go now?
  3. What examples must the speaker give to prove this point?

- Listen for ideas "between the lines" and for signal words and ask these questions:

  1. What is the speaker implying here?
  2. Why does the speaker stick to this one point?
  3. Is the speaker hinting at more than he or she is saying?

- Do your reading assignment before going to class.
- Take down main points of lectures in a lecture notebook, which is separate from the reading notebook.

HOW TO GET TWICE AS MUCH OUT OF READING

• • •

Putting Reading Skills to Work

Now let's put these reading skills to work for your child in another area.

Let's see how they can save time and effort every single day, how they can double the amount of information gotten out of a magazine or newspaper, and cut daily reading time in half. Let your child flash right through Shakespeare or Dickens, and dazzle class that very next morning with insights into scenes and characters.

Let's start with the number one source of information for most people—the newspaper.

How Professionals Read Newspapers

Your child needs two separate skills—two separate patterns of action—to get the most out of his or her daily paper:

Two Necessary Skills

134

1. How to read the newspaper as a whole.
2. How to read each individual news story
   that catches his or her eye.

First, let's set up an overall pattern of attack—a timed, step-by-step procedure—that will help tear out all the important facts from the paper every evening or morning.

Here's How Your Child Does it—Step By Step

1. When your child opens the newspaper in **Skim the** the morning, the first thing he or she does **Headlines** is skim all the headlines on the front page. (Or, if your house reads a tabloid, he or she should skim all the headlines of the first four or five pages.)

What your child is trying to achieve here—with this first rapid, overall view of the headlines—is "to see the world in one piece." To get a bird's-eye view of all the important events of the day at one time. *And to see—if possible—how each of these events ties in to others.*

For example, consider the week of Sep- **Bird's-Eye View** tember 15, 1996. Scanning the typical newspa- **EXAMPLE** per, your child would see that Nationalists sweep Bosnian elections . . . that Russian President Yeltsin is seriously ill . . . that more United States troops go to Kuwait . . . that the Virginia Military Institute admits women for the first time . . . that Dole and Clinton battle for the presidency of the United States.

Now, what does this bird's-eye view show? First of all—change! Other countries and our country are changing internally. They in turn can affect each other. But exactly how? How rapidly? Toward what?

- *How do these events tie in to each other?*
- *Is there a connection between President Yeltsin's serious illness and the Bosnian elections?*

- *If so, what is the connection?*
- *What effect could both these events have on the American election?*

This first two-minute glance tells your child what happened on that day, and leads him or her to set up questions about newspaper reports, and what effect one situation will have on the other. Your child now reads to answer these questions:

How to Read a News Story

2. Now your child starts on the articles them-selves. The objective here is to get the big facts—the important facts—out of each story as fast as he or she can, without missing a single vital detail. Your child does this by going back to the headline and turning it into a series of questions.

Get the Big Facts

More U.S. Troops to Kuwait

Headline EXAMPLE

This headline brings these questions to mind:

- *Why?*
- *How?*
- *When?*
- *How many?*
- *What will happen next?*

Virginia Military School Allows Coeds

Headline EXAMPLE

This headline brings these questions to mind:

- *Who made the decision?*
- *Why did they vote to admit women?*
- *How was the decision made?*
- *How many women will be admitted?*
- *Will the school make program changes?*
- *Are there administrative changes?*
- *What will happen next?*

Now—with these questions in mind—your child reads the first paragraph of the story. The first paragraph is actually a complete summary of the story. It gives an outline of what follows. It should answer most of your child's questions—along with *Who? . . . What? . . . When? . . . Where? . . . Why? . . . and How?*

Now, in most stories, this first (or second, or third) paragraph should give as much information as your child wants to know. In other words, it should answer the questions—at least in outline form.

However, if your child wishes to gain more information on any one of these points, he or she reads on. Each of the paragraphs that follows should be an expansion of one of the main points summarized in the first paragraph. Your child skims each paragraph until that point is mentioned again, and then reads it carefully to pick up the details he or she wants.

To Gain More Information, Your Child Reads On

This way, there is no waste reading, and no waste time.

Four Steps to More Information

Your child simply:

a. Reads the headline.
b. Frames the questions he or she wants answered about the details in that story.
c. Reads the first one or two paragraphs to answer those questions.
d. And then reads on only to pick up details on those points which vitally interest her or him.

By using this system your child can get the guts of a story in a minute or two. And then he or she is ready to go on to step three.

Learn the Background Behind the News

3. Now—when your child has read the important news of the day, and its important

Understand What It All Means

details—he or she turns to the sections of
your paper that tell:

• *What does it all mean?*

Now your child gets the comment of skilled interpreters to unravel
this news and help with his or her own opinions. So your child next
reads the columnists whose job it is to assign meanings to these
events.

And then your child turns to the editorial pages where the
paper itself interprets the news and takes stands on the major issues
of the day, and where readers like your child air their reactions in
their letters to the editors.

Get the Gist in Only a Few Minutes a Day

Now—how does your child pull out the gist of these many interpretations in only a few minutes each day? By reading them like this:

An editorial is built up differently from a news **Always Read**
story. In a news story the conclusion comes **a Column**
first; the details later. In an editorial, however, **or Editorial**
the writer begins by reciting facts you already **Backward**
know—by reviewing the situation to make it
fresh in your mind. And then goes on to state
his or her own conclusion. Or solution. Or
what this writer wants you to think and do.

So your child always reads a column or editorial backward. He
or she reads the last paragraph first, to pick up the writer's final interpretation.

Then your child jumps to the front. Skims rapidly through the
first paragraphs. Looks only for background facts that he or she
doesn't know . . . reasons to support his or her interpretation . . .
what the writer thinks will happen next.

Only a few minutes for each column, and your child is through
with the main news of the day. But look what your child has accomplished! *Your child has not only gotten the facts down solid, but
has formed his or her own opinions, and has plenty of good, solid,
clearly thought-through ideas to back them up!*

With this technique, your child will never be at sea in a serious discussion again. He or she will know exactly where to stand on important issues. Your child will think straight on crucial decisions—lead classmates' opinions on issue after issue.

Your Child Will Know Exactly Where to Stand on Important Issues

And Now Your Child Goes On to Finish the Paper

4.   Now your child turns to the index. Reviews the minor stories. Picks out the subjects of special interest—sports, business, style, home, what have you.

The Index

Your child uses the same headline-question-answer technique on each story he or she glances at. Pulls out the facts wanted—in minutes.

If your child reads movie or stage or book reviews, he or she uses the same last-paragraph-first technique used on the editorials. Your child gets the conclusion first. Then fills in interesting details.

5.   And when your child is through with the paper, he or she just doesn't throw it away and forget it. Your child thinks of the news as a continuing story. Follows each story as it develops day by day. Always tries to anticipate what will happen next.

Follow Stories Day by Day

6.   Your child should, if possible, read at least two different papers a day. Try to get different viewpoints. Compare them. Find out where they differ. Sharpen his or her reasoning power. Judge which one is right.

Different Viewpoints

7.   And, of course, have your child supplement papers with radio, TV, lectures, books, etc.

"Bonus Media"

Let's see how your child puts one of these "bonus media" to work—in half the time he or she is using today.

How to Flash-Read Magazines

With magazines, your child's plan of attack is different. Here's how to read them most efficiently:

1. Your child starts with the Table of Contents. Checks off the articles that interest him or her most. Turns their titles into questions, and then turns to them.

   Three Steps to Flash-Reading

2. Your child reads each article's title and subtitle . . . the first paragraph . . . all subheads . . . and the last paragraph or two. This should give the main idea, and enough information to tell whether to read further or not.

3. If your child does go further, again he or she asks questions before reading word by word. Remember—magazines present more than mere fact; they also give opinion. So, if your child comes across this kind of headline:

A Drug to Treat Cancer

Headline EXAMPLE

He or she asks these questions:

- *What is it?*
- *Who made the discovery?*
- *Is the discoverer qualified?*
- *What is the treatment required?*
- *How long would it take?*
- *What are its chances of success?*

4. Also, remember that most magazine articles are trying to get the reader to *feel, believe,* or *do* something. Therefore, your child asks:

   Find the Writer's Bias

   - *What reaction does this author want from me?*

- *How does he or she try to convince me that I should believe this?*
- *What facts or arguments are used to do this?*
- *What facts are distorted?*
- *What facts are left out?*
- *Where can I get the other side of this proposal?*

5. To help your child answer that last question, try to get him or her to read at least two magazines—with as contrasting viewpoints as possible. Have your child compare their interpretations. See what facts one leaves out that the other stressed. Your child forms his or her own judgments. **Contrasting Viewpoints**

6. Now your child skims through the article. Skips details. Gets the main thoughts. Goes on till answering his or her questions. And then turns to the next article.

7. When your child has finished the main articles of interest, then he or she quickly skims through the magazine, page by page. Your child may pick up something of interest that wasn't fully disclosed in the Table of Contents.

8. To read fiction in magazines, as in books, your child follows these rules:

How to Read Fiction Twice as Fast and Remember Twice as Much

1. Remember—*all fiction is about people.* Therefore, the first job is to get acquainted with the *people* in the book. **Identify the Main Characters**

Your child asks: Who is the hero? Then writes the hero's name on the inside front cover of **Who Is the Hero?**

the book. Describes the hero's appearance and character.

Who is the heroine? Your child writes her name. Describes her. Jots down the character traits and desires that are going to determine her actions throughout the book. **Who Is the Heroine?**

Who is the villain? Your child describes the villain. Lists the character's motives. Tells why they're going to bring the villain in conflict with the hero or heroine. **Who Is the Villain?**

Where are they all? Your child makes sure he or she knows the time and location of their surroundings.

What are they trying to do? What blocks them from doing it? *What's going to happen next?*

Make a list of *all* characters as you come across them. Keep adding to this list as you read the book. **Keep a Character List**

2.   Your child then reads the *first* chapters carefully. They set the stage—forecast the ultimate outcome. Then he or she can read faster and faster as the characters become more familiar—as the action becomes more predictable. **Find the Setting**

3.   Your child tries to outguess the author. The author has planted hints on what's going to happen at the end. Can your child predict that end before the author tells it to the reader? If your child can, he or she will not only get a tremendous kick out of it, but will learn how to see into people—predict what they'll do under stress. And this is the great benefit to look for from great fiction. **Predict What Will Happen Next**

4. When your child reaches the end, he or she asks: What happened? To whom? How did they change—for better or for worse?

    What is the author trying to say? What moral is being pointed out? What kind of world does the author say it is?

    Is it true to life? Does your child believe in the characters—in the events—in the outcome? This is the ultimate test. When your child has answered this question, he or she knows whether this work just read was great fiction or pulp fiction.

    And finally, what has your child learned? What has this author, in this book, taught your child about the way human beings act, feel, believe, fight, love, build, and even die?

    Never fool yourself. Your child can learn easily as much from fiction as from fact. And he or she can put these new insights—these new emotions . . . these new competencies in handling people—to work, the very same day!

    What Is the Moral?

5. Now, if possible, your child reads the reviews or textbook criticisms. Compares their judgments with his or hers. Searches for the *reasons* these reviewers give for their judgments. Then sees if his or her reasons hold up as well. If not, your child revises and strengthens them.

    Compare Book Reviews

6. And now your child turns to the back cover of the book. Sums up the entire book in one paragraph. Who did what—against what obstacles—and with what results? Your child tries to boil down the entire experience—the entire moral—into one

    Write a Summary

brief summary that will unlock the entire book again if he or she comes back to it even a year later.

For Advanced Students: How to Read Business Articles and Technical Reports

Business articles and technical reports have three main purposes:

- To report on work in progress.
- To detail particulars of some specific operation or method.
- To describe new and modern approaches to the problems of the profession or field.

Three Main Purposes

Therefore, to keep up with a particular field (or to conduct out-of-class research) with the least possible expenditure of time, they are read this way:

1. With a business journal, he or she follows the same first step as when reading any other kind of magazine. The Table of Contents is read first. Your child marks the articles of interest. Reads their summaries. Then decides if he or she will read them thoroughly.
2. In reading a technical report, however, the purpose must always be defined first. Your child must tell him or herself exactly why he or she is reading it and exactly what to look for. Then everything else must be disregarded.
3. Don't let your child be fooled by their formidable appearance. Their organization is usually quite simple. First he or she reads the title. Then looks for a summary—usually in the first paragraphs or the last.

How to Read Business Articles

4. Your child disregards footnotes. In nine cases out of ten, they're only for specialists in their field.

5. Your child concentrates on getting the main ideas. Numbers them. If the report describes a new procedure, he or she looks for each important step. Numbers them.

6. Your child should be able to boil down each report, each article, into a main-idea summary no longer than an index card. (If your child wants to keep the details, then he or she saves the article. Files it with reference to the index card.)

   After your child has boiled it down, he or she turns the index card over and tries to repeat its contents from memory. Your child tries to get every numbered point in the proper sequence. This gives a stronger grip on the article's organization—burns its main points into memory.

7. *Now your child decides what to do with that information.* Should he or she put it to work? Use it in a report at once? File it for future research? New information means new ability—new power—new competence. In the long run—if put to use—it means future prestige and money when your child leaves school and begins to carve a career.

Put It to Use!

✏ IN SUMMARY ....

Your child can double the amount of reading he or she gets done every day—and remember twice as much of it—by following these simple rules:

1. *Look before leaping.* Get the main idea first. Don't start reading word by word till you know the main idea. **Look Before Leaping**

2. *Ask questions.* Read to answer them. Stop reading when you have gotten the answers. **Ask Questions**

3. *Skip details.* They'll only confuse you while reading—slip out of your mind as soon as the page is closed. Concentrate on the core. Number it. Memorize it. **Skip Details**

4. *Then put it to work.* Remember—new knowledge means new opportunity—in school and out of it. **Then Put It to Work**

To the Student: Do It Yourself

Newspaper reading is the best start for practicing reading skills:

- Learn two patterns of newspaper reading:
  1. Reading the newspaper as a whole by getting a bird's-eye view through skimming all the headlines.
  2. Reading individual news stories by a question-answer technique. First set up questions that lead to main ideas in each news article when you find the correct answers.

- Read newspapers to answer your *why, how, when, what, how many* and other questions that will give you needed information.
- Skim each newspaper paragraph until you find your answers or main points, skipping unimportant details.
- For editorials, read the last paragraph first to get the writer's final interpretation.
- Use your new knowledge.

Magazine reading needs these different techniques:
- Look at the Table of Contents and check off the interesting articles.
- Turn the titles of these articles into questions.
- Skim each article for your answers, which are the main thoughts, by reading the title and subtitle, the first paragraph, all subheads, and the last paragraph or two.
- Then skim the magazine, page by page, to find something of interest not found in the Table of Contents.

Fiction reading requires a special focus on people.
- Ask the important questions:
  Who is the hero?
  Who is the heroine?
  What is the time and location of the story?
- Read first chapters carefully, predicting the outcome of the characters' lives. Later chapters will be faster reading.
- At the end of reading the novel, ask:
  What happened?
  To whom?
  How did the characters change?
  What is the author saying?
  Is the story true to life?
  What have you learned?
  Can you sum up the book in one paragraph?

For business journals, you follow the techniques of reading magazines.

For technical reports, take the following steps:
- Define your purpose.
- Read the title.
- Look for a summary.
- Find, number, and memorize main ideas.
- Now boil down each report into a main-idea summary that can be put on an index card. Decide if you want to use this information or file it for future use.

Expressing the Facts in Writing

CHAPTER 13

NEATNESS AND LEGIBILITY

• • •

The First Essentials

The most evident and measurable product that students sell in school is the daily paper they write. Though many schools no longer teach handwriting, the appearance of the papers handed in to teachers will, in their minds, be just as much a part of the students as the clothes they wear. Therefore, papers should be given just as much thought and attention by students' parents.

But this kind of care—neatness and precision on every single paper handed in—pays another huge dividend. *It will automatically, by itself alone, eliminate about 20 percent of the errors sloppiness would otherwise force students into.*

It will eliminate mistakes in addition, subtraction, multiplication, and division that might otherwise cost a downgrading from an A to a B. We will discuss this in detail in our section on mathematics.

It will eliminate mistakes in English, history, social studies, and other compositions that might irritate teachers so much that they could no longer concentrate on the content of the paper, and thus mark the work on the basis of the weaknesses rather than the strengths.

Yes, if you can permanently instill a sense of neatness, precision, and correctness in your child, you can boost grades by a full 20 percent. *And it is so incredibly simple to do.*

The procedure is a cinch. It consists of four steps.

1. A check on your child's present papers, to **Four Steps to** detect major errors in handwriting or- **Neatness** typing.
2. The correction of handwriting errors by practicing the correct way to do what the student is doing wrong today.
3. A constant, brief-glance check every night, to see that the old errors don't creep back in.
4. A check on your child's typing skills. Make sure he or she knows how to correct mistakes on the keyboard. Insist that he or she proofread everything carefully before printing it out.

Now, leaving neatness in mathematics to a later chapter, let's examine the most common handwriting errors your child might make today, and see how easy it is to correct them.

The Thirteen Fatal Errors in Handwriting and How to Correct Them

1. Fails to Dot *i*'s or Cross *t*'s

EXAMPLE:

The dog hit its right toe

How to Correct: Just use perseverance. Make sure every *i* and *t*, in every word, is finished off correctly.

2. Has Irregular Slant

EXAMPLE:

How to Correct: Use the following slant guide under your child's writing paper until he or she automatically slants each letter correctly.

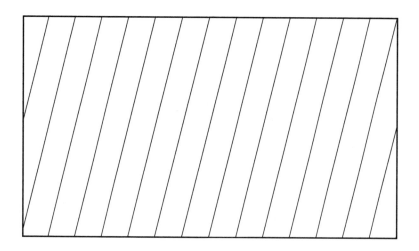

3. Spacing Is Uneven

EXAMPLE:

spacing uneven

How to Correct: Insist on a space equal to the width of a small letter between words. Don't allow your child to crowd the letters in each word together. There should be white space showing between every two letters.

4. Letters Are Irregular in Size

EXAMPLE:

Letters are irregular

How to Correct: All small letters should be exactly the same size and height, with capitals and loop letters twice as high. To instill this habit, have your child write on lined paper, like the following, till it becomes second nature.

a b c d e f g h

5. Writes Uphill or Downhill

EXAMPLE:

writes uphill or downhill

How to Correct: Again, use ruled paper to control wandering, until the habit of writing in a straight line becomes automatic.

writes uphill or downhill

6. Loop Letters Are Too Thin or Too Fat

EXAMPLE:

loop letters

How to Correct: Loops should be open, but no wider than an ordinary small letter. Long stems should be kept straight and not curved, as shown in the next example.

7. Stems Are Not Straight

EXAMPLE:

stems are not straight

How to Correct: Stems are the backbone or straight downward strokes, which are part of most letters. They should be written as slanted parallel lines, like this:

b b d g h i j k l

8. Fails to Close Letters

EXAMPLE:

doesn't close

How to Correct: Letters must be closed carefully at all places indicated by the arrows below. There should be no open spaces at all.

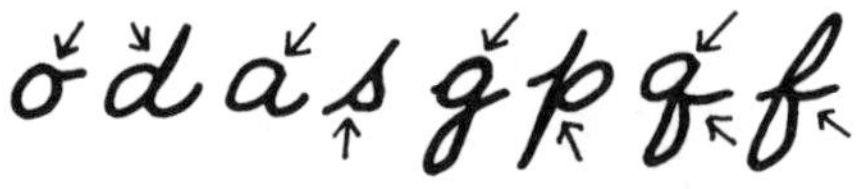

[handwriting example: o d a s g p g f with arrows]

9. Makes Pointed Letters Where They Should Be Round

EXAMPLE:

[handwriting example: The wind machine is mine]

How to Correct: Letters like *m, n, v, u, h,* and *y* have rounded tops or bottoms. They should not come to a point. To correct, have your child slow up a little when coming to such letters.

10. Does Not Retrace Properly

EXAMPLE:

[handwriting example: t m i u d]

How to Correct: Retracing means carefully writing over a part of the letter that you have made before. Worst offenders are *d* and *t.* See that each retracing looks like a single line.

11. Endings Are Too Individual

EXAMPLE:

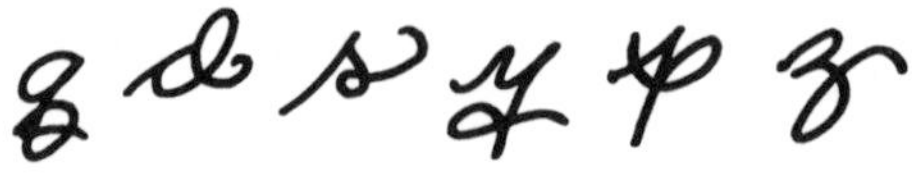

[handwriting example: g d s y p z]

How to Correct: Make sure the endings come no higher than those of a small letter, and eliminate any unnecessary curves in them.

12. Makes Sloppy Capital Letters

EXAMPLE:

Capital Letters Give Me

How to Correct: There are several styles of good capital letters. Have your child select one of them and stick to it, until he or she can write that style simply and well. Remember, fancy flourishes went out with the nineteenth century.

13. Writes Lines in a Slanting Column

EXAMPLE:

When in the course of human events it becomes necessary for a people to sever the economical and polit- ical bonds connecting it to another people, and affirm before God the

How to Correct: Place a rule down the left-hand column of the page, and have your child make sure that every first word in every line touches it.

In all of these common errors, *practice* is the only sure cure. With practice and careful checking on your part, your child will develop the habit of neatness and precision. And with precision, higher grades must automatically follow.

IN SUMMARY ....

Neatness and legibility are the first requirements of the successful student. They breed correctness. And correctness alone can improve your child's grades by as much as 20 percent.

To improve your child's neatness and legibility, adopt this simple three-step procedure.

1. Check present work, to detect handwriting errors. **Improve Neatness in Three Steps**
2. Correct those errors by practice in doing them the right way.
3. Recheck each night, to guard against errors creeping back in.

To the Student: Do It Yourself

- Raise your grade 20 percent automatically, by having work handed in neat and precise.
- Check your papers for handwriting or typing errors, by yourself or with a parent or relative.
- Practice the correct way to write these errors.
- Check papers every night to see that the old errors don't creep back in.
- Review the thirteen most common handwriting errors and learn to correct them. They are:

  1. Failure to dot *i*'s or cross *t*'s.
  2. Irregular slants.
  3. Uneven spacing.
  4. Irregular-size letters.
  5. Writing uphill or downhill.
  6. Loop letters that are too thin or fat.
  7. Stems that are not straight.
  8. Unclosed letters.
  9. Pointed letters where they should be round.
  10. Improper retracing.
  11. Endings that are too individual.
  12. Sloppy capital letters.
  13. Lines written in slanting columns.

We will now see how the same procedure, plus a fascinating trick, can wipe out spelling errors almost overnight.

CORRECT SPELLING
MADE EASY

• • •

Using the Three-Step System
to Improve Your Child's Spelling

In later life, when your child is submitting a résumé for an important job or writing an application for graduate school, a single mistake in spelling can ruin the entire impression he or she is trying to make. Even if someone works on a computer that has a spell-checker, there is no substitute for correct spelling.

There is no passing grade in spelling beneath 100 percent. It must be perfect. And it can be, if a student is taught to follow these simple rules:

The Wrong and Right Ways to
Improve Spelling

In the first place, *don't* try to improve a student's spelling by asking him or her to go over lists of misspelled words and correct them. These lists only concentrate attention on the *wrong* spelling.

Instead, focus efforts on the *right* spelling, in the *right* way, like this:

160

Realize that the reason someone misspells a word is because he or she has a *distorted image* of that word in mind. Your job is to help get rid of that distorted image, and replace it with the correct one in such a way that it is burned forever into your child's memory.

You do this in three simple steps:

First, you make the student *see* that word in such a way that *the correct spelling of the hard part of the word* sticks out like a sore thumb. **Three Steps to Correct a Misspelling**

Second, you give the student *spell-alikes* for the hard part of the word that bring the right spelling of it automatically to mind every time.

And third, you have the student write that word *twice as large as he or she ordinarily writes,* until the correct *feel* of the word is forever implanted in the muscles of his or her arm.

Not only are these three correction steps simple and easy, they are also enormous fun. Let's see how each of them works:

Step One: *See* the Hard Part of the Word Correctly

As you know, most words that are misspelled are misspelled in only one place in the entire word. Either your child has added a letter where it shouldn't be, or forgotten one where it should be, or put in an *e* for an *a,* or doubled a letter when it should remain single, or some other simple mistake.

But once that distorted image of the word has developed, then it sticks in mind and gets misspelled over and over again, always in the same way, always in the same place.

From that moment on, there is a part of that word that your child automatically misspells. It is that *hard part* on which you now concentrate.

First, you check over your child's papers and pick out the misspelled words. Then you locate **Find the Hard Part** the hard part of each of those words—the one or two letters in it that are always misspelled.

And then you rewrite that word correctly— this time CAPITALIZING those hard letters.

Write the Hard Part Like This:

- climB
- boRRow
- UNable
- paraLLel
- tomoRRow
- arGUMent, and so on.

Now you let your child *see* this capitalized correct spelling. You ask your child to copy the correct spelling on a sheet of paper—*with the capitals in exactly the same place that you have put them.*

Have that word written over and over and over again—capitals and all—until he or she has got it down pat. Until your child can see the correct capitalized spelling of the hard part of that word *with both eyes shut.*

Then you've completed the first step. Your child is on the way to perfect spelling.

Step Two: Build an *Automatic Memory Prompter* to Spell the Hard Part of the Word Correctly

Now you are going to reinforce that correct picture image of that word in your child's mind. You are going to do it by providing a simple *spell-alike* to help remember how the difficult letters go.

You are going to create an *automatic memory tie-in* between the difficult part of the word and an easy-to-remember spell-alike, like this:

There are three different ways to create these spell-alikes. Try them in the following order, until you get one that your child automatically remembers.

First of all, look for *familiar words within the hard words,* to make them easy to remember. Make up little sentences that tie these familiar words and the hard words together. For example:

Find the Familiar Words Within the Hard Words

- The SECRET was kept by the SECRETary.
- After I ATE, I was grATEful.
- We will GAIN a barGAIN.
- It's VILE to allow special priVILEge.
- Scientists LABOR in a LABORatory.

Second, if there are no familiar words within the hard words, then look for *the same part* in smaller familiar words. For example:

Look for the Same Part in Smaller Words

- We write a lettER on our stationERy.
- When we PARt, we sePARate.
- Please BRing the umBRella.

Finally, if neither of these first two rules works, then make up pure spell-alikes—as funny and as nonsensical as possible. For example:

Make Up Your Own Spell-Alikes

- She screamed EEE as she passed the cEmEtEry.
- GM uses good judGMent.
- I HANDed HER a HANDKERchief.
- I say BR when I think of FeBRuary.

There is a spell-alike for every misspelled word. One of these three rules will turn up the right one. Remember, keep them as vivid and as funny as possible: in that way, they'll be much easier to remember.

And, once your child is on to the game, let him or her think up the spell-alikes. It's not only great fun to see who can come up with the most outlandish ones, but it's marvelous training for future creativity.

And, always, it makes the correct spelling of those difficult words *automatic,* as soon as the spell-alike flashes into mind to suggest the way those hard letters should go.

Step Three: Get the *Arm-Feel* of Writing That Hard Word Correctly

Now, after you've capitalized the hard part of that misspelled word, and after you've both thought up a spell-alike to remember its correct order automatically, then your child is ready to *build the correct spelling of the word into a written reflex* without even thinking about it.

Here's how:

Have your child take a piece of blank, unruled paper and write the word in his or her natural script, without the capital letters, across the top of the paper. But have it written TWICE AS BIG as ordinarily.

TWICE AS BIG, over and over again. Have your child write it without looking at it. And without hesitating. Never stopping in the middle. If your child gets the word wrong, run through the first two steps again. And then go back to the TWICE AS BIG writing immediately.

Over and over again. Until your child builds the writing of that word into a mechanically perfect skill. Until that word is gotten down letter-perfect. Until it can be written correctly as casually as he or she writes his or her own signature.

Then it belongs to your child—forever.

How to Make This Three-Step System Work Every Day in School

To learn a new word, as we have said before, means to know its meaning, its use in a sentence, its correct pronunciation, and its correct spelling. Until all these are letter-perfect, your child doesn't really own the word at all.

As your child advances through school, he or she will meet more and more important new words. Some of them will be misspelled. Therefore, your child should have a Spelling Section in the back of his or her notebook.

Have this section divided into two parts. He or she should title the first part "Misspelled Words," and mark down in it any misspelled word.

Every night, have your child take one of these misspelled words—no more—and use the system to teach him or herself its correct spelling.

Then, when that word is letter-perfect, let him or her list it in the second part of the Spelling Section under the title "Mastered Words."

When about ten or twelve of these mastered words are listed, dictate all of them in a short paragraph or story. Then check each of their spellings.

If any are misspelled, put them back in the first part of the section, and start all over again. Because the correct habit hasn't yet been established.

But it will be. Before you know it, you'll be amazed at the absolute precision your child shows in these spelling tests.

And once a word has been mastered, encourage him or her to use it as often as possible. This practice will help to keep the correct spelling fresh in mind. It will also build confidence—show over and over again that your child no longer has the slightest reason to be afraid of misspelling that once-terrifying word.

Note also, spelling skills are no less important when your child is working with a computer word processing program. Your child should never rely on a spell-checker alone. These programs may be a good aid, but will not help when your child has keyed in a word that *sounds* like the word he or she wants, but is spelled completely differently (and has a different meaning), e.g.: read for reed, etc.

IN SUMMARY

There's only one permissible grade in spelling: 100 percent, letter-perfect.

This can be easily done if your child corrects every spelling error, individually, with this simple three-step method:

1. Detect the one or two letters in each difficult word that always get spelled wrong. Then CAPITALIZE the correct spelling of those letters till they stick out in front of your child's eyes like a sore thumb.

2. Think up *spell-alikes* for the hard letters that are automatic reminders of the correct way those hard letters should go.

3. And then give your child the *feel* of his or her hand spelling the word right, over and over and over again, twice as big as life, till it gets jotted down correctly as easily and as automatically as writing his or her own name.

This three-step system, applied daily to master one misspelled word, will make your child a spelling whiz in far less time than you believed possible.

To the Student: Do It Yourself

- Make a list of the words you have misspelled on your recent papers.
- Compare these words to the dictionary spelling and rewrite the correct word, capitalizing the letters that are not correct.
- Make up sentences with *spell-alikes,* described above, to remind you of how these words are spelled.
- Write the correct word over and over again, twice as large as usual, to familiarize yourself with the correct spelling.
- Each time you misspell a word and your teacher or a parent or relative corrects it, add it to your list. Once you acquire the habit of recognizing and correcting your spelling, your problems will disappear and good spelling habits will take their place.
- Be sure you have a good dictionary as a reference, to look up the words if you are not being helped by a teacher or parent.

WRITING
MADE EASY

• • •

How Students Can Write as Easily and Quickly as They Think

In their school career alone, students will be required to hand in at least four different kinds of written work: daily papers, research reports, themes, and examinations.

In addition, when they grow up, they will enter a world where they will be required to prepare résumés, interoffice memos, engineering reports, business and social letters, e-mail, and much more.

All of this vital work will be written. All of it will require that they be able to set down thoughts, suggestions, goals on paper or screen—so clearly and so persuasively that those papers and printouts serve as their best salesmen.

In this world, therefore, the ability to write well will be equally as important as the ability to speak well. People must be as fluid with the pen and keyboard as with the tongue. They must be just as much at home writing a school theme as telling a friend about a ball game.

In addition to the help computer word processing programs can give, students must develop *ease in writing on paper.*

167

Ease in writing and precision in writing come from two sources, both of which are available to your child:

- *Practice*
- *Planning*

It is the combination of these two that constitutes power-writing. Let us see how you can build both of them into your child, starting with practice.

How to Make Writing Easy for Your Child from the Beginning

Your child should practice writing as soon as he or she can spell out words on paper. Computers can also be useful in making early spelling exercises and writing efforts enjoyable and interesting.

The fact that a six-year-old can read words in the primer, or can painfully spell each of them out on paper or screen, really means very little. The child is using those words only passively; they do not yet belong to him or her.

What you have to do is help your child put those words to active use by showing how to combine them into written sentences and then linking these sentences into stories.

This, among all your work, will be the most rewarding. All children love stories. They love to hear them. And, given the chance, they love to write them.

Why not start your child on such an imagination game of writing? Here's how easy it is:

Give your five-, or six-, or seven-year-old child a list of dramatic phrases. They can be any words that will spark the imagination. For example:

A broken bicycle. An old man. A crooked road. Two children.

From such phrases as these, let your child weave a story. It does not have to be long, of course, or perfect. Just a paragraph or two of sentences leading from one event to another.

It will take only a few minutes to write. It's fun. And it will teach your child all these vital techniques:

1. How to arrange thoughts in order, so that one thought logically follows another.
2. How to divide each of those thoughts into a simple sentence, and then link those sentences up into a story.
3. How to put those sentences down on paper or screen both neatly and beautifully.
4. How to put the new words learned in school into active use, so they become a coordinated part of a working vocabulary.
5. How to spell those words correctly, and get the feeling of writing them correctly.
6. How to develop imagination and creativity, to be able to go from a few general hints to a fully developed tale.

The Six Techniques

Thus each one of these stories *puts together* the grammar and spelling and handwriting and word building your child has learned separately in class, *and makes them serve one dominant purpose— the expression of your child's own individual personality.*

Watch Writing Skills Grow

Give your son or daughter one of these story assignments every week. If he or she makes mistakes, carefully and constructively point them out and have the story rewritten correctly.

Then, with every story, read it aloud to the other members of the family; give your child pride in the powers of self-expression. And, as always, be lavish with your praise.

As your child grows older, start introducing stories about science, geography, history, and other subjects that he or she is becoming interested in school. But always, in these stories, ask for *original* ideas, *original* thoughts, *original* stories, and not the content of any book.

These simple weekly exercises, combined with the written work being done for school, will develop a youngster—before you know it—who can write as easily and vividly as the teacher.

And now, to build precision and power into that writing, you teach the equally simple technique of planning.

How to Decide What to Write, from the Beginning to the End

Like reading, and perhaps even more so, writing demands a plan of attack, a definite goal that your child wants to achieve in every composition, and a definite plan to get there—a series of questions that puts the student immediately on the right road, and keeps him or her there from the first written word to the last.

Let's look at such a series of direction questions right now. Let's work out a typical theme, and see how these questions and their answers avoid errors, strengthen the power of what is said, and cut writing time in half.

Let's take as our subject, *Should U.S. Astronomers Try to Communicate with Other Civilizations in Space?* This is a theme that a student might be asked to write in school any day. Let's assume that he or she answers the question with a "Yes," that the United States should try to send messages to other civilizations in the universe, and see how a student could develop this subject.

Questions to Ask Before You Start

- *What exactly am I going to write about in this paper?* (About whether U.S. scientists should attempt to communicate with other civilizations in different solar systems.)
- *Can I express this key idea in a single sentence, before I begin to write?* (Yes. "Scientists should try to communicate with other civilizations.")
- *How much am I going to say about it?* (I'm going to list the reasons why astronomers should do this.)
- *What am I NOT going to say about it, because I don't have the*

room? (Two things: (1) I am not going to list any arguments for the other side, why scientists should not try to communicate with other solar systems; and (2) I am not going to discuss any of the technical problems that we'll have to overcome to do this.)

- *What specific points am I going to make about this idea?* (The specific reasons why we should communicate with other solar systems: Because if there are other living beings out there, we can let them know of our existence. Because we can show them we are intelligent. Because we can indicate we are peaceful. Because it will enable us to look for clues about whether other civilizations exist. And because it fulfills man's destiny to explore the universe.)
- *How many of these points are there?* (Five.)
- *In what order should they be arranged? Which should come first, second, third, and so on?* (In this order: First, we can reveal to them our own existence; second, we can show them we are intelligent; third, we can show we are peaceful; fourth, we can learn about them; and fifth, we can increase exploration.
- *Which of these points are the most important; which should be given separate paragraphs?* (All of them.)
- *Which points should I group into one paragraph?* (None.)
- *What is the best way to catch my reader's interest?* (Probably with a strong, emphatic assertion at the very beginning. Something like this: "There are at least five vital reasons why the U.S. should try to communicate with other civilizations in space, any one of which would more than justify this project's cost.")
- *How do I end? Can I think of a good last sentence before I begin to write?* (Yes. A summary sentence something like this: "Therefore, to keep our scientific research from falling behind, to maintain our prestige with other nations of the world, to receive the benefits from otherwise overlooked scientific discoveries, and to assure the United States' leadership at the forefront of human destiny, it is essential that this country try to communicate with other civilizations.")

How Students Can Perfect Their Compositions Before Starting Them

The questions outlined above give your child **Benefits of** two major benefits. They force him or her to **the Outline** choose a definite, easily handled topic, clearly formulated, concrete, and specific, with no chance of wandering over its chosen limits. And they help him or her write about this topic one step at a time, with each step in its proper place.

Without such a blueprint, a student simply won't know where he or she is going, and revising a paper will take more time than originally writing it.

Now, once students have the answers to these questions, they arrange them quickly in a Main-Thought Outline, just as they do in their daily reading. The process in both reading and writing is the same, but it is done in reverse. In writing, students get their main thoughts first, build them into an outline second, and then write the paper itself on the basis of that outline.

They write the title for the paper across the **How to Build** top of the outline: *"Why the U.S. Should Try to* **an Outline** *Communicate with Other Civilizations in Space."*

Students write the first sentence directly below this title: *"There are at least five vital reasons why the U.S. should try to communicate with other civilizations in space, any one of which would more than justify this project's cost."*

They take their first major idea and mark it with the Roman numeral I:

I. To keep our scientific research from falling behind.

If this first major idea demands more than one paragraph to explain it fully, students then mark each one of these paragraphs with the capital letters A, B, C, and so on:

I. To keep our scientific research from falling behind.
   A. To keep our scientific knowledge from falling behind.
   B. To keep our scientific curiosity from falling behind.
   C. To keep our scientific technology from falling behind.

Each of these paragraphs will have several sentences within it, to develop important details. These detail sentences are marked in the outline by Arabic numerals, and are placed under the capital letter paragraph to which they belong. For example, in paragraph A above, students would have these detail sentences:

A. To keep our scientific knowledge from falling behind.
   1. Will force us to develop more imaginative research tools.
   2. More powerful communications systems.
   3. More powerful telescopes.
   4. And therefore more ability to gather information.

They continue on, developing every major idea in this way, marking them with the Roman numerals II, III, IV, and so on. Then breaking them into their separate paragraphs, and marking these with the capital letters A, B, C, and so on. Then outlining the individual detail-sentences with Arabic numerals 1, 2, 3, and so on, till they have finished outlining the entire paper.

Students then write in the concluding sentence and they are finished with the outline. Here is a brief sample of what that outline will look like at this stage.

WHY THE UNITED STATES SHOULD TRY TO COMMUNICATE WITH OTHER CIVILIZATIONS IN SPACE

There are at least five vital reasons why the United States should try to communicate with other civilizations in space, any one of which would more than justify this project's cost:

1. To keep our scientific research from falling behind.
   A. To keep our scientific knowledge from falling behind.
      1. Will force us to develop more imaginative research tools.
      2. More powerful communications systems.
      3. More powerful telescopes.
      4. And therefore more ability to gather information.
   B. To keep our scientific curiosity from falling behind.
   C. To keep our scientific technology from falling behind.

II. To maintain our prestige with other nations of the world.
   A. More scientific publications.
   B. More highly educated people.
   C. More international scientific awards.

III. To receive the benefits from otherwise overlooked scientific discoveries.
   A. Research facilities.
   B. Manufacturing plants.
   C. Testing and feedback.
   D. Space education.

IV. To assure U.S. leadership at the forefront of human destiny.
   A. To prevent other nations from luring away all our scientists.

And so on, until the outline is finished.

How to Write the Final Draft

From this point on, the final draft of the composition writes itself.

The student takes the title and the first sentence and puts them down on the paper. He or she then takes main idea I and phrases it into the next paragraph, like this:

First of all, of course, such a project is necessary to keep our scientific strength from falling behind that of the rest of the world.

Now the student takes each of the three paragraphs under this main idea I, and builds them according to the outline, like this:

In our comparative scientific strength alone, the intergalactic communications project will yield vast benefits. It will force us to develop more powerful communications systems. It will force us to devise larger and more accurate instruments to work them. These better instruments will give us more information, which, in turn, will help us develop even more scientific expertise.

The same exact benefits will be felt in our other astronomical programs. From the communications project research, we will gain better instruments. We will develop more sophisticated computer systems, with faster speeds and greater accuracy. And we may even find ourselves with a network of communications systems spread across the universe.

And so on. Paragraph by paragraph, right through the entire paper.

When the student is through, he or she will have a composition that develops the subject thoroughly, that presents the points in logical, persuasive order, that makes good reading and makes sense, and that earns top grades.

Tips for Developing Clarity and Power

1. Every paragraph should contain only *one* main idea and the details that develop it. When students go on to discuss a second main idea, they should start a new paragraph. **One Main Idea Per Paragraph**

    This has been shown over and over again in the examples above.

2. Each sentence, in its turn, should contain only one idea. The great mistake most students make is in trying to crowd too many ideas into a single sentence. This results in huge, clumsy, poorly graded sentences. When you get to a second idea—or when **One Idea Per Sentence**

you find two or more ideas crowded against each other in a single sentence— separate them and make each into its own sentence.

After we arrived home from the trip, tired and dirty, we immediately went upstairs, where we unpacked our clothes and hung them up, before we allowed ourselves to take a shower and go to bed.

EXAMPLE: Wrong Way

We arrived home from the trip, tired and dirty. We immediately went upstairs. After unpacking our clothes and hanging them up, we took showers and went to bed.

Clearer and More Powerful Way

3. Long sentences in school compositions are usually confused sentences. One sure way to avoid this mistake, and to write clearer, stronger sentences, is to keep the subject and predicate of each sentence as close together as possible.

Keep Subject and Predicate Close Together

The man whom Tom had seen earlier that day running away from the bank spun around when he saw Tom.

EXAMPLE: Wrong Way

The subject of this sentence is "man" and its predicate is "spun." The reason the sentence is confusing is that this subject and predicate are separated so widely by the clause "whom Tom had seen earlier that day running away from the bank." Therefore, to make these two thoughts far more powerful and clear, they should be separated like this:

It was the man whom Tom had seen earlier that day running away from the bank. When he saw Tom again, he spun around.

EXAMPLE: Right Way

4. Make sure your child's sentences are connected correctly. He or she has to point out the relation between one sentence and the next. Otherwise, the reader won't know where the train of thought is going.

   Connect Sentences with Transition Words

   Connecting words are *and, yet, but, so, or, for, however, therefore, thus, otherwise, because, from, such, this,* and so on. They point out to readers what the second sentence has to do with the first, what the third has to do with the second, and so on.

   A good exercise for your child would be to go through a few pages of any good book and underline the connecting words the author uses. Have him or her bring the book to you after underlining a page or two in this way. Ask exactly how each connecting word ties in one sentence with the sentence that goes before.

   Exercise

   This way, your child will develop skill in using these tie-in words, and his or her papers will be a powerful procession of closely woven thoughts.

5. Your child must learn to carefully proofread and review the entire finished composition word-for-word. Spelling, repeated words, awkward phrases, correct usage of vocabulary in context, overall sense and meaning—all must be checked one last time before the work is ready to be handed in. It bears emphasizing that a misspelling of one word is often the correct spelling of another, so a spell-checker will not detect it. For example, a spell-checker would find nothing wrong with: "Won mourning lass

   Proofread and Review

tweak, eye lead the glass in the Pledge or Allegiance." Only the writer of the sentence would spot all the mistakes.

☞ IN SUMMARY ....

The ability to write well is as important as the ability to speak well, and it is as easy to learn.

Ease in writing comes from two sources: practice and planning.

In regard to practice, your child should start to write compositions as soon as he or she can spell words on paper or screen. Your child should write one a week for you, from the first grade on.

He or she should also be taught, from the very beginning, the principles of planning. Before starting to write a word, your child should already have defined the subject, the main thoughts, and the opening and closing sentences.

And he or she should have arranged them in paragraph-by-paragraph order in a Main-Thought Outline, so the paper will practically write itself when your child sits down to begin it.

To the Student: Do It Yourself

- Practice using words in sentences, and then linking these words into stories.
- Write at least one composition a week.
- Have your parents or relatives read over your compositions and discuss them with you. See whether they have understood what you were trying to say.
- If they did not, perhaps you were not making yourself clear. Rewrite the composition if this is the case.
- Plan your writing:

  1. Define your subject, your main thoughts, and your opening and closing sentences.
  2. Arrange your thoughts in order, so that one thought logically follows another in a Main-Thought Outline.
  3. Divide each of those thoughts into a simple sentence, and then link those sentences up into a story.
  4. Put those sentences down on paper or computer screen both neatly and beautifully.
  5. Put any new words you learned in school into active use, so they become a coordinated part of your working vocabulary.
  6. Spell those words correctly, and get the feeling of writing them correctly on paper.
  7. Develop imagination and creativity, to be able to go from a few general hints to a fully developed tale.

Mathematics Can Be Fun, If You Do It This Way

16

MATHEMATICS MADE EASY

. . .

How All Parents Can Help Their Children with Math, Even If They Can't Add Two and Two

Unfortunately, most parents, like their children, are awed by mathematics. They realize that it produces more school failures than any other subject. They have unpleasant memories of it from their own classroom days. They believe that it consists of nothing more than brain-twisting problems, with no relation to everyday life, done for the amusement of super-eggheads in ivory towers.

Nothing, of course, could be further from the truth.

When you get right down to it, the basic principle of all math, from arithmetic to calculus, is as simple as ABC, and as practical as a screwdriver. It can be stated in one clear sentence:

Mathematics is THINKING BY STEPS to solve problems.

Just that, and nothing more. Math is the art of solving problems, STEP BY STEP. The key is STEP BY STEP.

Even the most complicated problems can be broken down into one simple step following another. Once you teach your child this secret, you have shown him or her how to lick math.

183

How Step by Step Works

Let's take a closer look at this basic principle.

Math is simply a *way of arriving at correct answers* when you are given a certain set of facts called a problem. It is *thinking by steps* to get from what is given to what is asked for. It is the art of solving a problem, *one easy step at a time,* to reach the correct conclusion.

Approached in this way, math becomes not only simple, but fun. More fun than solving crossword puzzles or riddles, but developed step by step in exactly the same way.

It is within the reach of every child—and every parent. For even if the technical problems themselves may be beyond you, the simple method of arriving at their correct answers is easily within your supervision and control.

What This Section Will Do for a Student

Any parents, even if they cannot add two and two, can help their children in three vital, *nontechnical* areas of math, where 90 percent of a good start lies. These three areas are:

1. Preventing careless mistakes, which rob most children of 20 percent of their mathematics grades every day. Neatness and precision are very important. Chapter 17 will show you how to cut out this waste 20 percent overnight.

    Three Vital Areas to Help Your Child

2. Making abstract parts of problems as real to your child as his or her own thumb. Chapter 18 will show you how to do this with a few quick lines of your pencil.
3. Unraveling complicated word problems and proceeding step by step to the correct answer. Chapter 19 will show you how to make even the longest, most involved problem nothing more than a series of

easy steps that your child can do in one-two-three order.

But first, right now, let's take a look at a few hints.

Basic Hints for Top Grades in Math

1. No matter how bright your child, there are **Memorize the** certain fundamentals that must be memo- **Fundamentals** rized so thoroughly that instant correct results are given back to you every time. For example, the addition and multiplication tables.

    Here, there is no substitution for *drill.* No substitution for *practice,* over and over again, in cars, at the dinner table, before going to bed, and when brushing hair every morning.

    Over and over again. When your child is alone, in the classroom, or with you. The right answers must become so second nature that there is no counting, no picking or scratching with a pencil, no moving of fingers or lips till your child tells you the right answer.

2. As this mastery of fundamentals is built **Find the Problem** up, and as his or her recitations give you **Numbers** the feel of what the mathematical strengths and weaknesses are, you will notice that certain numbers give more trouble than others. For example, number 9 is a troublemaker for most children, in addition, subtraction, and multiplication. But your own child may have his or her own particular bogeyman—6 or 5 or 7.

    In any case, watch for that troublemaker. Identify it as soon as possible. Then give special drills to eliminate it. Keep pounding at it, over and over again, till it becomes as automatic as all the rest.

3. In any kind of math, from the most simple **Master a Step**
   addition to the most complex calculus, **Completely**
   each new step builds directly on the step that **Before Going On**
   came before it.

   For example, your child must learn to add one and one before learning to add two and two.

   Must master the addition table before learning to multiply.

   Must master the multiplication table before learning to
divide.

   And must be completely in control—foolproof and mis-
take-proof—in addition, subtraction, multiplication, and division—before beginning to think of learning algebra or any
other branch of higher mathematics.

   Each step builds on the step that came directly before it.
Therefore, your child must completely master that first step be-
fore going on to the second.

   And must understand each of those steps—each of them in
turn—so completely that it becomes second nature. And only
then can your child go on to the next.

   To do this, *practice* is a must. He or she must do sample
problems for each new step. Go over and over them. Eliminate
any possibility of confusion or mistake. Never let your child
leave any classroom with any problem or process unclear in his
or her mind. Have your child question and requestion the
teacher till he or she understands it completely.

   Again—*practice.* The same day-after-day practice that is devoted to mastering other skills—sports or music or dance. For
every new step learned in any course in mathematics, he or she
must practice.

   Then and only then will the next step in the course be as easy
as the one just finished. Only then will your child be able to zip
right through those math courses, without constantly being lost
and bewildered, constantly being forced to backtrack and learn
again something that should have been mastered the first time.

4. Because one step depends so completely **Keep a Math**
   on the step that went before it, your child **Notebook**

has to pay special care to the math note-book. It must contain:

a. A basic vocabulary of every new term learned in the course. That term must be listed alphabetically, defined in a sentence, and illustrated with a sample problem and a solution showing how it applies to the problems that will be given in the tests.

b. A listing of every single new operation learned in the course (for example, how to add fractions that total less than one; how to add fractions that total more than one; how to add whole numbers and fractions together, and so on). Each new operation should be named, and accompanied by a sample problem and solution showing each step in the solution broken down in the exact correct order.

c. A mistake page listing every error that has been made in previous exams and the correct method of solving it. For a thorough discussion of this all-important point, see Chapter 20.

5. And because of this dependence of one step upon the step that came before it, sickness or an accident that causes your child to be absent from class is a far greater problem in math than in any other subject. **Make Up Missed Material Before Going On to New Material**

In math, your child must make up the steps missed when sick, before ever beginning to understand the work the class is doing when he or she returns. You have to get your child to understand that lost material—immediately, in order not to fall further behind.

This means night work. If you can, teach it yourself. If you can't, see if the teacher will give after-class help. If the teacher can't do this, then get a tutor at once.

Again, *drill* your child. Pump in that missing information, and test, test, test. You'll know he or she has caught up when the daily classroom papers come back to their previous standard. And don't settle for anything less. This is important even in this day and age when calculators are commonplace. Calculators cannot take the place of knowledge of math.

IN SUMMARY ....

Math can be made easy for your child once he or she does it the right way.

The vital secret to be learned is to do the math problems *step by step*. And to master one step before going on to the next.

Your child does this by learning three simple techniques:

1. Neatness and precision, to make sure your child gets every step down right, without a single unnecessary mistake.
2. Translating abstract steps into concrete terms that can be easily understood.
3. Unraveling complicated word problems so your child can automatically do them, one simple step at a time.

To the Student: Do It Yourself

- Thoroughly memorize mathematical fundamentals, such as addition and multiplication tables. Drill them till you know them without thinking.
- Think of math as step-by-step thinking, with each step building on the step before it.
- Because each step builds on the step before it, you must completely master each step before going on to the next one.
- The way to master each step is by practice, practice, practice.
- Be sure you understand each new process or problem before you leave your classroom. If you do not, question and re-question your teacher until he or she explains it so you understand. *This is especially important if you have been absent.*
- Be sure your notebook is complete and clear. It should contain:
  1. Alphabetical listings of all new terms introduced in the course, with one-sentence definitions and illustrations.
  2. Alphabetical listings of all new operations introduced in the course, with sample problems and solutions, in step-by-step order.
  3. A listing of all your errors in previous exams which includes the correct way to solve these problems.
- Try to avoid the carelessness that is responsible for reducing your mathematics grades by 20 percent.

Let's now examine these techniques, one by one.

HOW TO AVOID
MATH ERRORS

• • •

One Simple Secret for Avoiding
20 Percent of All Math Errors

It is a proven fact that careless mistakes, sloppy copying, slips of the pen, and just plain inattention account for approximately 20 percent of all errors in mathematics.

Think of this fact for one moment. If your child is now bringing home, say, a 70 on math papers, simply substituting precision for sloppiness in doing the work could improve that grade—overnight—20 percent, or 14 points, or bring the work up to an 84.

One simple demand on your part—for neatness, accuracy, precision—will make that much difference. *Isn't it worth a few minutes of your time, right now, to teach your child these three fundamental rules that can result in one-fifth better grades overnight?*

Precision Rule Number One:
Write Each Number Legibly

Most students scrawl their numbers rather than write them: 4's look like 9's or 7's; 2's are mistaken for 3's. Error is built into the work at the very beginning, and your child never has a chance to overcome it.

Your first task, therefore, in building precision into your child's math is to check each one of the ten numbers he or she writes down on paper. Every one of those numbers must stand out sharp and clear, without the slightest chance of a mistake, even to a casual glance.

Here are the most common errors students make in writing numbers, and the correct way each numeral should look:

1   2   3   4   5   6   7   8   9   0

(handwritten numerals) / 𝒳 𝟥 4 𝟧 6 7 𝟪 9 0

Make every number as legible as it is on the printed page, and your child has taken a giant step to better math grades in a few short minutes.

Precision Rule Number Two: Place Columns of Figures Exactly Under One Another

The second great careless error that robs your child of top math grades is a zigzag column. A single number allowed to wander out of position is a sure guarantee that the problem is going to be done wrong.

Make sure your son or daughter places all numbers in precisely the right position in every problem. The columns of figures should form straight vertical lines—with the 1's precisely under each other in the 1 column, the 10's in the 10 column, the 100's in the 100 column, and so on.

There is a simple way of checking to see whether this is being done right. Take a ruler and draw lines between the columns of figures. If the lines do not touch a single numeral, the columns are correct. If they do, then have your child recopy the problems again until they are right.

Here is a typical sloppy column in addition, and the same problem written correctly. You can see the difference at a glance.

$$
\begin{array}{r}
7\texttt{\$}54.72 \\
3.02 \\
103.07 \\
70.27 \\
259.36 \\
47.00 \\
\hline
161.73
\end{array}
$$

Precision Rule Number Three: Copy Each Problem Correctly

No child can get an answer right without first having the problem right. The problem has to be copied out of the book, or off the class blackboard, and onto the paper precisely. A single figure miscopied can trigger a tailspin of confusion for a full hour, while the student is trying to find out where it went wrong.

Therefore, your child must learn the vital technique of copying correctly. Here's how it goes:

Four Steps to Correct Copying

1. Your child copies word for word, number for number. Nothing is left out, nothing is condensed, nothing is abbreviated. Every mark that is on the board should be on the paper, in exactly the same position.
2. When your child has finished copying the problem, he or she should check each line, and then the problem as a whole, in this way. First, the number of lines in the problem on the board are counted; then the

lines on the paper are counted to see if they match. Then the contents of each line are checked, one by one, to make sure each figure matches. Only then does the work begin.

3. On word problems, your child underlines each of the key words in the problem on the paper (see Chapter 19 for a description of *key words* in mathematics). Then each key word is checked with the board to make sure he or she has them all, and they are all correct. Only then does the work begin.

4. At the end of the solution, if the answer does not seem reasonable, it's time to check the problem against the board once again. Your child may now spot a miscopied figure that he or she had overlooked before. And this may save precious moments of wrestling to correct a wrong answer whose error had lain in a miscopying at the outset.

IN SUMMARY ....

Approximately 20 percent of all errors in math are caused by miscopying or misreading numbers.

Without absolute precision in every step made in mathematics, your child is beaten from the beginning.

This vital precision is gained by learning three simple techniques:

1. To make sharp, clear numbers that can't be mistaken even at a quick glance.
2. By making ruler-straight columns, with each number precisely in the right place.
3. By copying the problems exactly—photographically—with every number exactly as it is given.

To the Student: Do It Yourself

- Be careful and you can improve your grade by 20 percent.
- Write each number correctly at all times. Write it neatly and precisely. Double-check to be sure you did.
- Be sure all the numbers of all your columns line up EXACTLY.
- Make double certain you copied the problem CORRECTLY from the book or blackboard. Check that you copied it correctly again before going on to try and solve it. Check each line, then the whole problem.
- Underline the key words in the problem, then check to make sure you have them all, and they are correct.
- If your answer does not seem reasonable, check the problem against the board again to make sure you copied it correctly.

Once this habit of precision has become second nature, your child is then ready to learn how to make abstract problems as plain and as simple as one's thumb. We now turn to this technique.

HOW TO TEACH MATH WITH PICTURES AND MODELS

• • •

Making Abstract Ideas Concrete

One of the most difficult parts of mathematics for most children is the fact that it is abstract, that it deals with ideas that children cannot see or touch or picture easily in the mind's eye.

Therefore, these abstract ideas become hard for children to work with, *when they would really be quite easy if someone just made them into physical pictures or models to see.*

Most parents instinctively recognize this fact. When you taught your child how to count, for example, you did not ask him or her to try to add the abstract number "one" with another abstract number "one" to get the abstract number "two."

Instead, you offered *physical objects* to add—one *ball* with another *ball* to make two *balls,* or one *marble* with another *marble* to

195

make two *marbles*. Only later did your child learn to separate the numbers from the objects and add one and one of *anything*.

The same rule—the same construction of physical models—holds true throughout students' entire school career. From time to time, they are going to be introduced to new abstract ideas. They are not going to be able to see or touch or picture them immediately. And they are going to have trouble with them for this reason alone.

Therefore, your job is to give them physical models that make these ideas easy to work with.

Let's look at some of the most common of these abstract ideas. Let's see how easy it is to turn them into pictures or models they can see and move around, once they're given the key.

Let's start with one of the hardest ideas to picture in grade school, one that causes most people most trouble throughout their entire lives.

How to Make Pictures of Fractions

A *fraction* is a part of a whole. This is its word definition, but it is extremely hard to picture. So let's work with fractions, not only with words and numbers, but with pictures.

The fraction 1/4 looks like this:

1/4

The complete box represents a whole, or the number 1. The fraction 1/4 is one-fourth of that whole box. Your child should learn to shade the fraction (in this case, the 1/4), to make it stand out from the remainder of the whole.

You may also draw a picture of 1/4 without representing the whole box that it is a part of. You do it in this way:

1/4

Now, once you learn the idea of making these fraction pictures, working with fractions becomes as simple as adding or subtracting building blocks. Let's take a few examples:

Adding Fractions the Picture Way

Suppose students are given the problem: Add 1/4 + 1/4 + 1/4.
They immediately draw this picture:

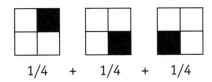

1/4   +   1/4   +   1/4

Notice that each 1/4 is shaded in a different part of the whole box. This makes adding easier in the final answer.

Of course, the answer is now perfectly evident, even at a glance. It is:

= 3/4

It is as easy as counting blocks. And it remains that easy, even when students go on to more complicated problems that might otherwise have given them weeks of trouble. Like this:

Reducing Improper Fractions the Picture Way

An *improper fraction* is a fraction that adds up to more than one, and should therefore be changed to a whole number and a proper fraction. For example, students may be given this problem:

Change the improper fraction 9/4 to a mixed number. (A mixed number is a whole number and a proper fraction, in this case 2-1/4.)

To do the problem, students first lay out the 9 fourths, like this:

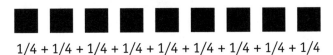

1/4 + 1/4 + 1/4 + 1/4 + 1/4 + 1/4 + 1/4 + 1/4 + 1/4

Then they simply group them into wholes, as easily as assembling blocks, like this:

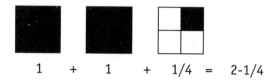

1   +   1   +   1/4   =   2-1/4

The answer is as plain as the noses on their faces: 2-1/4. It's simply a matter of grouping and counting physical units that they can see and touch.

Of course, they use these pictures only until they understand fractions so well they become second nature. Then they automatically drop the models—just as they dropped the balls and marbles of their first countings—and use the now-mastered abstract idea of fractions to go on with.

One more example will make this clear.

Adding and Subtracting Fractions with Different Denominators the Picture Way

A *denominator* is the part of the fraction that   **Denominator**
is under the line (the /4 in 1/4, the /2 in 1/2, and
so on). To add or subtract fractions with different denominators, students may be given a
problem like this:

> *If Susie and Ted need 1/2 yard of cloth for one art project, and 1/4 yard for another, how much cloth do they need in all?*

They can easily solve this by remembering that 1/2 looks like this:

1/2

And 1/4 looks like this:

1/4

So added together, they form this picture:

= 3/4

Thus different denominators become as easy to work with as problems having the same denominators.

But as students grow more at home with fractions, they can forget about drawing pictures for each problem, and go on to the faster way of working with the different fractions themselves.

To help them do this—to help them picture the relation of many different denominators at once—you give them a new model. This time it is a Denominator Chart, like this:

1															
1/2								1/2							
1/4				1/4				1/4				1/4			
1/8		1/8		1/8		1/8		1/8		1/8		1/8		1/8	
1/16	1/16	1/16	1/16	1/16	1/16	1/16	1/16	1/16	1/16	1/16	1/16	1/16	1/16	1/16	1/16

Notice that you are still working with pictures, but this picture is more abstract than the blocks you were building before. Thus you are moving the students step by step to mastery of the truly abstract principles of mathematics, but giving them complete understanding and self-confidence every step of the way.

Other Math Models You May Build for Your Child

Decimals are hard for most children only be- **Decimals**
cause they don't realize that they've been
working with them all their lives, in the form of
dollars and pennies.

A penny is a decimal part of a dollar (one-hundredth, or $.01).
So is a dime (one-tenth, or $.10). So is a quarter (one-fourth, or
$.25). Train your children, at least at the beginning, to substitute the
word *pennies* for *decimal points* when they begin to solve decimal
problems.

Thus the problem "What part is .25 of one?" becomes "What
part is 25 cents of one dollar?," which they can answer instantly.

All other decimal problems are equally a cinch, once children
think of them in terms of money.

Percentages are just multiplying by pennies. A **Percentages**
percentage is nothing more than a decimal
with the period in front of it removed and the
percent symbol (%) placed after it. Thus 10%
is equal to .10. And your children already
know that .10 equals $.10 or 10 cents.

Thus 10% = .10 = $.10 = 10 cents.

Percentages are used to multiply other numbers by. If you want
to find 25% of 100, you multiply 100 by 25%, or .25, or have a "bankruptcy sale" where you're only going to get 25 cents on the dollar. Thus
25% of 100 is 25.

This image of a "bankruptcy sale" makes percentages quite easy
to do, for the simple reason that it turns the abstract idea of "percentages" into physical dollars and cents. Try it for a while with your
child. The results may amaze you.

Algebra may be thought of as a game, a series **Algebra**
of riddles in which someone hides a number
and your child has to find it.

The number that's hidden is replaced by a letter of the alpha-
bet. For example, $x = 2 + 3$. To find x, simply add 2 + 3.

The puzzles get harder as the game goes along, but the rules are still the same. Letters are substituted for numbers, and they have to be rearranged, step by step, in order for numbers to be found.

Thought of this way, algebra becomes quite simple, and quite a lot of fun.

Geometry

Geometry was invented to solve physical problems—engineering problems, building problems, farm problems. Later, it lost this solid nature and became quite abstract. Your job is to make it physical again. You do this by building, or helping your child build, models. Triangles made of matchsticks. Circles made of string. Rubber balls serving as spheres. Physical objects that your child can measure, open and close, compare one with the other.

This is especially important in solid geometry, where it is practically impossible to understand the course without physical models. Here, five minutes spent taking apart and putting together a plastic model of, say, a cylinder, will be worth two hours of abstract book study.

IN SUMMARY ....

Some of the most important ideas in math are abstract—extremely difficult to see or touch or picture clearly.

Because they are abstract, these ideas are hard to work with until somebody makes them solid and real.

This is done by using pictures and models of those ideas. This chapter has listed several physical models that you can easily give your child.

These models help students grasp the fundamental idea easily and quickly. Later on, when it has become second nature, they will no longer need the model, and will be able to work directly with the abstract idea itself.

To the Student: Do It Yourself

- Note the picture used in this chapter for 1/4. Practice it until it becomes second nature.
- Make pictures for 1/2, 1/3, 1/5, 1/8, and 1/16. Practice these as well.
- Try making other models that can be used in algebra and others that can be used in geometry.

Now we show students how to apply almost the same technique to break complicated problems down into a series of simple, easy-to-do steps.

HOW TO SIMPLIFY MATH PROBLEMS

• • •

Making Complicated Problems Half-Solve Themselves

In the first four years of their school careers, students will concentrate on the fundamental skills of addition, subtraction, multiplication, and division.

Starting with the fifth grade, however, and continuing past college and throughout adult life, if they pursue a business or engineering or scientific career, they will be presented with far more complicated problems.

- Problems that involve as many as a dozen or two dozen individual steps.

Complicated Problems Abound

- Problems that are given out of order, and must be rearranged before they can even begin to be solved.
- Problems that are stated in words as well as numbers, and demand reading as well as figuring.

These complicated word-and-number problems *cannot,* of course, be solved by blindly rushing into them. Like any other studies, technique is demanded in order to simplify and organize them.

Not one, but three separate skills are required in order to master them:

Three Techniques to Simplify and Organize

1. Reading
2. Reorganizing
3. Problem solving

Let's examine these techniques, one by one.

Why Are Word Problems So Hard for Your Child?

First, because they involve several steps. They are actually several little problems in one.

Five Reasons Word Problems Are Difficult

Second, because they demand reading skill as well as figuring skill. Students must understand every word of the vocabulary they are reading. And they must be able to pick out the key parts of the problem by using that vocabulary.

Third, these parts of the problem are often not presented in the order that must be followed to solve them. Thus, after they are first read and understood, their order must be reversed so that each part of the problem can be solved in its proper turn.

Fourth, often there is a "hidden problem" that makes up one of the parts, which is never even stated at all. This "hidden problem" must thus be identified, stated by the student, and then solved—all in its proper place.

And finally, since all these sub-problems are stated in words, there are no plus or minus signs to tell students what operations to perform. Where, in number problems, the correct operations are given by the signs, here they must furnish them themselves.

How to Overcome All of These Obstacles with One Simple Technique

Because of all these complications, procedure—step-by-step attack—is vital for word problems. Choice of method is crucial. The wrong procedure not only has a fifty-fifty chance of coming out wrong, but it will probably take five to ten times as long as the right method.

For example, take this typical grade-school problem:

> If apples are sold at *two for five cents, how many*   **Sample Problem**
> can be bought for *eighty-five cents?*

Step One: Read the Problem

The first thing students do, of course, is actively read the entire problem, word by word, slowly and carefully, with pencil in hand.

All the skills they have learned in reading come into play here. For unless they read the problem correctly and understand it completely, nothing else they do can give a right answer.

In fact, a leading educator at Columbia University has said this: "In advanced math, precise reading is actually 90 percent of the battle."

Therefore, students *double-read* the problem. They read it the first time to get its overall meaning. And then they read it again to underline the key words.

When they have finished, the problem looks like this:

> If apples are sold at <u>two for five cents, how many</u>
> can be bought for <u>eighty-five cents</u>?

Step Two: Ask, What Is Given?

Now, when they have understood the problem completely and marked the key facts, they ask: "What is given? What does this problem tell me? What are the facts I have to start with?"

In this case, the facts are simply that apples are sold at *two for five cents*.

Step Three: Ask, What Is Called for?

Ask, "What answer is called for?"

In this case, "*How many* apples will *eighty-five cents* buy?"

Step Four: Ask, Is There a Hidden Question? If So, What Is It?

In this case, the answer is, yes, there is a hidden question. It is, "How many times does five cents go into eighty-five cents?"

Step Five: Ask, How Many Steps Are Needed to Solve This Problem?

Now you decide how many little problems there are in this big problem.

In this case, there are two:

1. Finding out how many nickels there are in eighty-five cents.
2. Finding out how many apples this number of nickels can buy when every nickel buys two apples.

Step Six: Find Out What Operation Must Be Done in Each Step

Now find out whether to add, subtract, multiply, or divide.

In Step 1, you must divide 5 cents into 85 cents to get the number of nickels.

In Step 2, you must multiply the answer from Step 1 by two apples to get the final answer.

Step Seven: Make Sure the Steps Are in the Right Order

You must ask, "What do I need to do first? What do I need to do second?" And so on. Then, if necessary, you must rewrite the problem in the correct order to solve it.

In this case, the steps are already in the correct order.

Step Eight: Do Each Step in Turn

In this case:

$$1) \ 5\overline{)85} \ \ \begin{array}{c} 17 \\ \hline \\ -5 \\ \hline 35 \end{array} \ = 17$$

$$2) \ 17 \times 2 = \underline{\underline{34}} \ apples \ for \ 85\cancel{c}$$

    You must, of course, remember to use the answer found in Step 1 as one of the figures in Step 2.

    And when you find the final answer, you should not only write it down but underline it.

Step Nine: Check the Answer to Make Sure It's Right

Do this by reversing the two steps, like this:
    To check Step 2:

$$2\overline{)34} \ \ \begin{array}{c} 17 \\ \hline \\ -2 \\ \hline 14 \end{array} \ = 17$$

To check Step 1:

$$\begin{array}{r} 17 \\ \times 5 \\ \hline 85 \end{array} = 85\cancel{c}$$

    You now have the right answer, and you know that answer is right. Make sure to follow this simple procedure for every word problem encountered, and you'll be amazed at how easy they all become.

How to Turn "Hopeless Problems" into Snaps

Word problems are one of the two great bogeymen of advanced mathematics. The other terror of the classroom is the long, complicated problem involving half a dozen to a dozen steps.

Most children freeze up when given an involved problem that doesn't resolve itself into a simple, easy answer, or that takes a long series of steps.

But these problems are just as easy as 2 + 2 = 4, if your child only *works them out one step at a time,* and writes down each of the answers.

The secret is simple: *hard, complicated problems are just a lot of easy problems strung together.*

Therefore the trick in getting students high grades in higher math courses is simply this:

Make them see that a hard problem can be broken down into a series of simple, easy steps.

Make them do these problems one step after another, each in its proper order, and each written down on paper.

The procedure is simple. The problem is broken down into a series of steps. Each step is taken in turn, and written down on the workpaper. No step, no matter how simple, may be omitted. No step may be done in a student's head, or placed on another sheet of paper.

Each step is written out, solved, and the solution used to help solve the next step in its turn.

This way, students eliminate the three major nontechnical sources of error throughout their entire use of higher math.

Eliminate These Three Sources of Error

1. They don't take crazy shortcuts that can trip them up in a dozen different ways.
2. They don't strive for quick, done-in-the-head answers that aren't thought through.
3. *They concentrate on the PROCEDURE by which they get the answer,* and not on the answer itself, which comes automatically out of that procedure.

In Math, *Method* Is the Key to Success

In mathematics, strange as it may seem at first glance, the correct answers are not nearly as important as the way your child arrives at them.

The means—the methods—the procedures your child learns in math classes are the real treasures carried away into later life. Individual problems and answers come and go. But the correct procedures will continue to give thousands of correct answers, all through life.

Therefore, remind students over and over again that the great value of a correct answer is that it shows they know how to use the correct procedure.

Emphasize mastery of method. This leads the mind away from fruitless copying of correct answers. It focuses attention on getting the procedure right today, so that it can automatically give the correct answer every time.

What to Do If a Problem Has Your Child Stopped Cold

One last hint. All students, no matter how bright, run into a problem from time to time that just stumps them. In this case, there is a simple procedure that may break that roadblock immediately. Here it is:

Seven Steps to Breaking Roadblocks

1. Have them read it again from the very start. They should look especially for clues that they may have missed before. It may even be helpful to have them rewrite the problem again on a fresh sheet of paper.
2. Go over the steps. A simple error in addition may have thrown them off.
3. Try substituting simpler numbers for those given in the problem. If it is a problem in algebra, try restating it in arithmetical numbers. This may make it simple enough

to see the correct procedures to be followed at a glance.

4. Have them go on to the next problem for a moment. This may supply the needed mental connection.

5. Let them leave the problem for a night. Then perhaps they can solve it the next morning when their minds are fresh, and they've had a chance to absorb the procedure.

6. Look up a similar problem or procedure in another book. Perhaps a new author's way of explaining the problem will make it clear.

7. If nothing else works, be sure the student discusses the problem with the teacher the next day. Check back that night to make certain it is now completely understood. Follow the Golden Error procedure outlined in the next chapter.

IN SUMMARY ....

Complicated math problems are made simple in these two ways:

If It Is a Word Problem, Follow This Nine-Step Procedure:

1. Read the problem.
2. Ask what is given.
3. Ask what answer is called for.
4. Ask if there is a hidden question in the problem. If so, ask what it is.
5. Ask how many steps are needed to solve the problem.
6. Find out what operation must be done in each step.
7. Make sure the steps are in the right order.
8. Do each step in turn.
9. Check the answer to make sure it's it's right.

If It Is Not a Word Problem, but Is a Long, Complicated Problem with Many Steps, Follow This Procedure:

1. Break each problem down into a series of steps.
2. Do each step in turn.
3. Write every part of every step down on the workpaper, omitting nothing.
4. Use the answer from one part to help get the correct answer from the next.
5. And so on until the problem is finished and right.

To the Student: Do It Yourself

- Approach word problems step by step.
- First, read the problem two times, once for overall meaning, again to underline key words.
- Then ask yourself what is given.
- Ask what answer is called for?
- Ask if there is a hidden question in the problem, and if so, what is it?
- Ask how many steps it takes to solve the problem?
- Figure out whether to add, subtract, multiply, or divide.
- Make sure your steps are in the correct order.
- Do each step in turn.
- When you find the answer to each step, underline it.
- Check each answer.
- For hopeless problems,
    1. Break them down into simple steps.
    2. Do one step at a time.
- Don't take crazy shortcuts.
- Don't do quick, done-in-the-head, unthought-out answers.
- Remember that procedure—method—is most important.

(continued)

To the Student: Do It Yourself *(continued)*

- If a problem really stumps you:
  1. Read it again and write it out on a separate sheet of paper.
  2. See whether you've missed anything.
  3. Go over the steps. Check for errors.
  4. Try substituting simpler numbers to see if it becomes clear.
  5. Do the next problem, then come back to the one that stumped you.
  6. Leave it overnight and go back to it in the morning when you're fresh.
  7. Find another, similar problem in another book and see if it is explained more clearly there.
  8. If all else fails, discuss the problem with your teacher.

Mastering Facts—

The Art of Remembering and Review

CHAPTER 20

HOW TO PUT ERRORS TO WORK

. . .

Errors: The Royal Road to Knowledge

Every student, no matter how bright or slow, learns some facts quickly and has trouble with others.

Those learned easily require little outside help. It is the troublesome fact, the error-causing fact, the fact that blocks the road to understanding that we must concentrate upon.

The telltale symptom of trouble, of course, is a mistake in work. Most parents are worried by these mistakes. *They do not realize that if they are handled correctly, they are worth their weight in gold.*

Why? Because a mistake is actually nothing more or less than a signpost in your child's work that signals a misunderstanding.

And by analyzing what went wrong in each of those mistakes, and correcting it, you will help your child achieve a far deeper level of understanding and competence than can ever be gained without them.

This is perfectly in accord with the prime rule of all self-improvement—*work on weaknesses.* The strengths will always be there. But the weaknesses must be identified and gone over and over again until they are no longer there.

215

Let us therefore examine this technique of turning a mistake into gold. It is as simple as this:

How Your Child Can Profit from Mistakes

It is never enough for your child simply to glance at a daily paper when it is handed back, and notice that there is an error on it.

Every day, on every error, students must be able to answer these three questions about that error before they are allowed to go on to new work:

1. Where in the problem did you make the mistake? **Three Questions About Every Error**
2. What did you do wrong that caused you to make that mistake?
3. What is the correct operation that will avoid that same kind of mistake in the future?

Let's see how these three questions turn errors into accomplishments.

For example, let's say that a student came home with a wrong answer in a long-division problem. **Step One: Locate the Error**

The student knows that the answer is wrong, but where exactly did it go wrong?

Was it a mistake in multiplication or subtraction inside the problem?

Was it only one mistake or several?

The student should be encouraged to break the problem down into steps. Check each step to find out which one went wrong. Don't rest till you can pinpoint the exact step where each error occurred.

Now, when your child has located the exact spot where the error occurred, it is important to identify its cause. **Step Two: Find Out What Caused It**

Let's say that it was a mistake in one of the multiplications. Your child multiplied 6 by 9 and came up with 52.

What caused this mistake?

Was it simply carelessness? Or is that mistake a warning to the two of you that he or she is weak in multiplying 9's?

Step Three: Correct the Cause of the Error

If it was carelessness, review again the techniques of checking an answer to make sure it's right before it is handed in. And review Chapter 13 on neatness and legibility.

If, however, your child does show a weakness in 9's, stop everything and review the 9 section of the multiplication table. Do it over and over again until it becomes automatic, and automatically right.

Remember, you have to correct the cause of an error before you can permanently correct the error itself. If you do not correct the cause first, the error will simply repeat itself later on.

Step Four: Correct the Error Itself

Now take a fresh sheet of paper, copy the problem onto that paper yourself, and have your child work it again.

This time it should come out right. If it does, file it away and come back to it the following week. Give it to your child again on a fresh piece of paper.

If he or she gets it right again, enter it into the Mistakes Made page at the back of the class notes.

Step Five: Do Similar Problems to Make Sure the Technique Is Correct

At the same time, give the student several other problems with 9's in them. Concentrate on those 9's. Within a short time, he or she will have mastered them all and the correct answers will flow with perfect confidence.

IN SUMMARY ....

Follow this same technique with every step made:

- Break the problem down into steps.
- See which step went wrong.
- Find out why.
- Correct the cause of the error.
- Have your child rework the problem the right way.
- Keep her or him doing it over and over again until the right answer is absolutely automatic.

This way mistakes help rather than harm. You are helping your child climb from mere "good student" to champion. Because he or she won't make that mistake—or its first cousin—again. Because you have helped to remove a misunderstanding—a roadblock.

To the Student: Do It Yourself

- Break each problem down into steps.
- See which step went wrong.
- Find out why.
- Correct the cause of the error.
- Rework the problem the right way.
- Repeat the correct way again and again until it becomes automatic.
- This way, you can turn errors into achievements.

This process of turning errors into achievements is one of the finest forms of review. We now turn to a complete discussion of this all-important subject.

PLANT FACTS IN YOUR CHILD'S MIND

• • •

How Your Child Can Learn Facts and Never Forget Them

We are now ready to review what your child has learned so far in this book, and tie it together into one overall plan for mastering any subject given in school.

Mastering a course—any course—consists of the following logical steps:

1. Students find out what has to be learned in each assignment in the course.

   Six Steps to Mastery

2. They read that assignment to get at the heart of its meaning.
3. They write that core meaning down in their notebook, in a few brief sentences or phrases related to each other in the outline form.
4. They tie the outline of that assignment into the assignment that came before it.
5. They then review as much as they have studied of the entire book or course

EVERY WEEK, to get an overall view of everything that has been studied.

6. At the end of the term, a week or two before the final test, they then make a final review of their strengths and weaknesses throughout the entire course. Here they find out what they know well; what they should know better; what they really do not know at all.

And on the basis of this final review, they create the final study schedule for the week before the test.

This, then, is your child's Plan of Mastery for school subjects. We have already discussed Steps 1 through 4. We now turn to Steps 5 and 6—the strategy of review, of fixing the heart of the course permanently in mind.

What Review Is Not

First of all, let us define review by saying quite definitely what it is *not*.

Review is *not* cramming, *not* last-minute effort, *not* the desperate piling up of information in frenzied disorder.

This type of cramming always fails. It always has failed. It always will fail. Why? Because it attempts to store up large quantities of unorganized material. And without organization, there can be no memory. Material crammed into your child's brain leaks out again as fast as it goes in.

What Is Effective Review?

Boiled down to its essentials, active effective reviewing is nothing more or less than this:

Continuous self-examination—of the essential parts of a course.

Effective review, then, consists of these two essential steps:

Two Essential Steps to Effective Review

1. Boiling down the material of the course to its essentials, and then boiling the

essentials down again and again and again, till students have mastered every word of the core meaning of that course.

2. Periodically reviewing that core material—through continuous self-examinations—till every word of its content is right at the tip of their tongue, ready to be instantly formed into an answer.

For example, mathematics is thus reduced to rules, definitions, types of problems that will be encountered in the final test, and the formulas and procedures that will solve them. Then all this essential knowledge is rehearsed, over and over again, till the correct answer to any one of the problems becomes an automatic reaction.

This is the same combination of knowledge and practice that makes a champion linebacker, a top-flight golfer, or a superbly successful executive.

Once students have reviewed the course in this way—in other words, once they have reduced it to its essentials and practiced quizzing themselves on those essentials till they have become second nature—they are ready to breeze through any test that can be thrown at them on that subject.

Now, let's examine this process of review and readiness, step by step. There are three steps:

Three Steps to Review and Readiness

1. Weekly review.
2. Final organization of notebook.
3. Final quiz-review of the entire course.

Let's look at each one:

Step One to Effective Review: The Weekly Review

Effective review, of course, is not a once-a-semester activity. It goes on constantly, first as part of your child's day-by-day study, then to survey a larger area once every week, and then to insure understanding of the entire course at the end of the term.

We have already discussed, in Chapter 10, the first step in this continuous process. We went over the three questions your child uses to tie in each new chapter with the one that went before:

- *In one sentence, what did I learn from last night's chapter?* **Three Tie-In Questions**
- *How does this tie in with the chapter before?*
- *What questions will I be asked on it in next week's test?*

Now, at the end of each study week, students go one step further. Each week, they set aside one additional half-hour for review of the entire book up to that point.

During this hour, they review each chapter outline in their notebook. They then tie them together—in a continuously growing overall view of the book as a whole—with this series of questions and answers:

- *How many chapters have I now read in this book?* (Using the high school history book as our example: three, plus an introduction.) **Review with a Series of Questions and Answers**
- *What is the title of the book?* (*A History of Civilization.*)
- *Does this title give the theme of the book?* (It does.) If it did not, the student would then ask the question:
- *What is the theme of the book?* (A history of civilization.)
- *What, if any, is the title of the introduction?* ("The Uses of History.")
- *What, in one sentence, is the core meaning of the introduction?* (A study of history keeps us from making the same mistakes all over again that our ancestors made.)
- *What is the title of the first chapter?* ("The First Men.")

- *What, in one sentence, is the core meaning of the first chapter?* (Primitive man spent almost all his time getting enough food to keep alive, until he invented agriculture.)
- *What is the title of the second chapter?* ("The Near East.")
- *What, in one sentence, is the core meaning of the second chapter?* (The first great civilizations in history—ruled by kings and priests and resting on slavery—were built in the Near East.)
- *How does the second chapter tie in with the first?* (By showing the tremendous growth in civilization agriculture made possible, even though this civilization was enjoyed only by the few who had seized rule.)
- *What is the title of the third chapter?* ("The Greeks.")
- *What, in one sentence, is the core meaning of the third chapter?* (The Greeks developed the first Western civilization, inventing democracy, science, philosophy, literature, and so on.)
- *How does the third chapter tie in with the second?* (By showing the contrast between the older, king-and-priest-dominated civilizations of the Near East, and the new freedom that characterized Greek civilization.)

And so on. Chapter by chapter, every week of each course.

This weekly review pays off in several ways. It keeps the older chapters fresh in students' minds. It ties in each new chapter with the material that preceded it. It gives students an ever-growing overall view of the course. It helps them get higher grades in class recitations and weekly exams. It cuts down the amount of reviewing they will need to do in the last two weeks before their final exams.

And it helps them to simplify and to bring their notebook up to date, like this:

Step Two to Effective Review: The Final Organization of the Notebook

At the end of each course, when they are ready to begin their final review, students have in their notebook:

1. A *Main-Thought Outline* of every textbook chapter in the course.
2. A *Main-Thought Outline* of every lecture given in the course.
3. If there are any, *Main-Thought Outlines* of any outside reference reading assigned during the course, done in the same way as any daily reading assignment.
4. A *fundamental vocabulary page* for the course as a whole.
5. A *list of the mistakes* they have made in their daily papers during the progress of the course.

The Five Parts of an Effective Notebook

These five different notebook parts must now be brought together into a single final outline page for each chapter in the course.

They must be blended together with the duplicate facts removed. They must be arranged in a single, logical order, so that every fact they have learned during the course fits in perfectly, and can be remembered—automatically—the instant it is needed.

The Final Blending of Notebook Parts

Blending Step One: Blend Reading and Lecture Main-Thought Outlines

For each chapter, students take their reading notes and lecture notes (and, if there are any, outside reference notes) and lay them side by side.

Lay Reading and Lecture Outlines Side by Side

They then take a third sheet of paper and start to blend them in, point by point. They start with the chapter title, then the first main thought underneath that title, then the second, and right on down the line.

To help with this blending task, they ask themselves the following questions:

- *Is this fact repeated by both sources?* (If so, they throw it out.)
- *Is this fact new?* (If so, they put it under the proper heading in the revised outline.)
- *Do I have to change the order of my headings because of any new facts?* (Sometimes, when material from separate sources is put together, students will find that neither one of the older outlines can contain the blended facts. In this case, they must construct a brand-new outline and order containing all the new facts in their proper relation to each other.)
- *Are all these facts really important—are they really main thoughts—or are some of them merely details describing other main thoughts already picked up from another source?* (If so, they leave them out.)

These questions cause students to weigh and choose and reject. They make the mind work. In themselves, they are an excellent form of review. And when students are finished answering them, and shaping their answers into a final Main-Thought Outline, they will pretty well know everything there is to know about the material in that chapter.

Blending Step Two: Red-Check the Lecture Main-Thought Outline

Now, they go back over the lecture notes for that chapter, and ask themselves the following questions:

Red-Check Probable Test Questions for Final Review

- *What questions will my teacher be most likely to ask about this chapter?*
- *What points did my teacher stress in the classroom lectures?*
- *What information did my teacher tell us to pay special attention to in the textbook?*

Every time they find the answer to one of these questions in the lecture notes, they place a red check in front of that point in the revised Main-Thought Outline. This check will serve as a signal when composing the final review questions, as we will describe below.

They now throw away the reading notes, the lecture notes, and the reference notes. They have no more need of them, since they have been blended into the revised Main-Thought Outlines.

The Revised Main-Thought Chapter Outlines

Blending Step Three: Tie In the Fundamental Vocabulary Page with the Revised Main-Thought Outlines

Now they turn to the fundamental vocabulary page. They remove this page from the notebook and lay it alongside the revised Main-Thought Outlines for the course.

Find the First Use of All Key Terms

They go down the vocabulary, word by word, and check off the point in the Main-Thought Outlines where that word is first used in the course. At that point they make an asterisk (*) in the Main-Thought Outline, and then write the word and its definition at the bottom of that outline page.

They do this till they have exhausted every word in the fundamental vocabulary. They have then tied the vocabulary in with the notes, and gained a deeper understanding of both in doing it.

But they do not throw away the fundamental vocabulary page. They continue to carry it at the back of the notebook as an instant reference if they should forget the meaning of the words as they appear in more advanced lessons.

Blending Step Four: Review Mistakes

They now take out their daily or weekly written work, and check each one of the mistakes they have made during the entire course.

Wherever they have made a mistake, they place a red check mark against the same point in the Main-Thought Outlines. This again reminds them to pay special attention to that point in the final review.

They now have a completely revised and ready-for-review notebook. It contains every fact learned from the reading, the lectures, and the reference research, all blended together into one thoroughly understood stream of thought.

Revised and Ready-for-Review Notebook

In addition, they have incorporated into those outlines probable test questions, a thorough understanding of the vocabulary of the course, and review signals for every weak spot that has shown up in their work for the entire term.

Test Questions, Vocabulary and Weak-Spot Review

They are now ready to perform one final review operation on that notebook, which will thoroughly prepare them for the final test by enabling them to anticipate 80 percent or more of all the questions the teacher can give, IN THE EXACT FORM THE TEACHER USES TO PHRASE THEM.

Step Three to Effective Review: The Final Quiz-Review of the Entire Course

Let us say that your child has begun the final revision of the notebook two weeks before the final exam. It has taken one week to complete this revision, and thus to master the main thoughts of the entire course.

There is now one week left to prepare to breeze through that final exam. In the next chapter we will outline day-by-day, step-by-step procedures for that final week. Right now, however, we will see how students take revised notes during that final week, and turn them into a private test before the real test, to make sure they know every detail of that material.

There are two reasons, of course, why they take this private test:

1. Obviously, because it gives one final **The Private Test** chance to again review the material, to gain still deeper understanding of it and more confidence in handling it.

2. Because it is one thing to know the core material of a course, and quite another thing to be able to quickly and accurately answer test questions about it. To really whiz through a test, students should be familiar with the questions that are going to be asked on that test—not only their form, but their very content. And the only way to discover that content—outside of cheating—is to construct your own test out of

the same materials the teacher will use to construct it.

Therefore, students now begin to turn the revised notes into test questions, in this way:

How to Make Up Your Own Test Questions

As we mentioned in Chapter 10, each page of your child's notes is written on one side only. The opposite side is purposely left blank. That blank side is about to be put to work.

Let us say that students are going to review our sample chapter four, "Five Roads to Cost Reduction." They have already revised the outline notes, to include both text and lecture ideas into one overall outline. **EXAMPLE**

They now turn that sheet of paper over and write across the top of the blank side: *Five Roads to Cost Reduction—Test Questions.*

They are now ready to make up questions. In doing this, they must remember that, in the final exam, they will be given two general types of questions. **Exams Have Two Types of Questions**

- First, the *short-answer questions,* such as multiple-choice, true-false, fill-in, and so on.
- Second, the *essay questions,* which ask them to write a paragraph or more in answer to every question.

To prepare for both types of questions, students draw a horizontal line across the middle of the paper, dividing it in two. **Use a Graphic Example**

- At the top left-hand corner of the upper half, right under the overall title, they write: *Short-Answer Questions* **Short-Answer Questions**

- And at the top left-hand corner of the
  lower half, right under the dividing line,
  they write: *Essay Questions*

  Essay Questions

They now draw a vertical line down the middle of the paper, to divide the questions from the answers. The paper now looks like this:

Five Roads to Cost Reduction—Test Questions

Short-Answer Questions	*Answers*
1.	
2.	
3.	
4.	
5.	
6.	
7.	
8.	

Essay Questions	*Answers*
1.	
2.	
3.	
4.	
5.	

They are now ready to compose questions.

How to Make Up Short-Answer Questions

In Chapter 23, you will be shown each of the different types of short-answer questions, along with simple formulas to greatly aid your child in answering them.

Here we can touch on only a few of these types of questions, to use as examples of how your child should convert lecture notes into a final self-quiz, proceeding in this way:

First, of course, students take every point that the teacher has emphasized in lectures, and convert it into a test question.

Let's say, for example, that the teacher has stressed the methods of cutting capital equipment costs in the lecture. Students immediately construct a cross-out test question on this point, and use it as the first short-answer question on the page, like this:

Which of the following four procedures is NOT **Convert Points to**
a way to cut capital equipment costs? **Short-Answer**
a. Reducing costs of depreciation, replace- **Questions**
*   ment, maintenance, and interest.*
b. Holding down inventories.
c. Operations research.
d. Sharpening accounting procedures.

The answer, of course, is *c.* But they do not yet write in that answer. Instead, they go on to the next question.

This next series of questions revolves around those points that they have made errors on in previous work. For each error made, they now compose a self-test question.

For example, let's say they had difficulty be- **Compose a True-**
fore in remembering the ways to cut raw ma- **False Question**
terial costs. They now construct a true-false
question on just this point, in this way:

> TRUE OR FALSE: Three good ways to cut
> raw materials costs are: precise purchasing
> specifications, inspection of incoming ma-
> terials, and financial control of sources.

The answer, of course, is *True.* And so they go, down the entire list of important points, constructing a different question for every one of the types mentioned in Chapter 23. In this way, they become thoroughly familiar with each one of these question types, *as they apply to the material they will be tested on.*

They even use the same procedure to make sure they know the exact meaning of each of the words in the fundamental vocabulary. For example, suppose they want to be absolutely certain of the meaning of *Operations Research*. To test themselves on this point, they construct the following question:

Compose a Self-Test Vocabulary Question

> *OPERATIONS RESEARCH means most nearly:*
> a) Cost Accounting
> b) Statistical Decision Making
> c) Computer Planning
> d) Time and Motion Study

The answer is *c*. But the construction of such a question forces students to think deeply about the meaning of this new word, to compare and contrast it with the other new terms learned in this course, and to dig deeper into more and more profitable levels of understanding.

How to Make up Essay Questions

The same procedure holds true on preparing essay questions. They first go over the important points stressed by the teacher. Then the points they have been confused on before.

Then whatever other ideas they believe they will be tested on in the final exam.

For each of these they prepare an essay-type question, such as those described in Chapter 24.

For example, on manufacturing costs, a simple essay-type question would be this:

Turn Important Points into Essay Questions

1. *List five ways to cut manufacturing costs.*

Or, as a more complicated essay-type question:

2. *You have just been appointed sales manager of the ABC Company. Describe five*

*ways that you would attempt to cut sales
costs, in order, and tell why you think each
of these ways would be effective.*

How to Answer Essay-Type Questions on Self-Quiz Paper

When they have written all the questions—both short-answer and essay-type—down the left-hand side of the paper, the students are ready to take their own quiz and write the answers.

They do not do this the same day that they composed the questions. They wait a day, and then come back to the quiz.

Without looking at their notes, they write the answers. For the short-answer questions, they write the answers completely.

For the essay-type questions, however, they do not write a complete answer. Instead, they *outline* each of the answers as briefly as possible, and do not take the time to actually write in the outline as they would do in an actual test.

They are only trying to develop the main ideas for the answer, and the order in which they would arrange them. Once they have this, they can be satisfied, and go on to the next question.

For example, in essay question two, about the sales manager position, your child would outline the answer in this way:

WAY TO CUT COST	REASON WHY
1. Advertising	1. Biggest cost today
2. Warehousing	2. Greatest percent improvement
3. Transportation	3. Big waste in most co's
4. Direct Sales	4. Fat usually creeps in
5. New Specialists	5. May be cut entirely

How to Review the Self-Quizzes

Once they have taken the test, students grade themselves right or wrong, just as the teacher would. Those answers that are right they forget until the last day before the test. Those answers that are wrong they review again the next day, in this way:

They place a red check mark in front of the question missed. The next day, they take out the self-quiz again, cover the answer side with a sheet of fresh paper, and try to answer the question again.

If they get it correct this second time, they forget it till the last day before the test.

If they miss it again, they reread the notes, and then turn back to the original textbook material and reread it again. If they still do not understand it after this rereading, they immediately speak to the teacher about it, going over it until they are absolutely sure of it.

Remember, their goal—and your goal—is to make certain that they understand every important idea in the course well enough to allow them to answer any question on it that can be thrown. You can accept nothing less.

What These Self-Quizzes Will Do for Your Child

If they have done them correctly, when students are through with these self-quizzes, they have accomplished the dream of every student who has ever walked down a classroom aisle to take a final exam:

They will actually know the examination questions in advance!

You see, the teacher, in preparing the final tests, has no more material to choose from than your child. Both your child and the teacher will have to concentrate on the same broad ideas and important details as the sources for their test material.

Therefore, to a surprisingly large extent, they must come up with exactly the same questions.

Think of the thrill students will get when they march into the final exam room and finds dozens of the exact same test questions waiting there—*with the correct answers perfectly stored away in their heads, ready to spring onto the paper.*

Think of the head start this will give them over their more poorly prepared classmates. Think of the tremendous burst of confidence this will raise—to completely erase any nervousness they might have brought into the room with them, to carry them right through every question on the test, with the mind already revved up to full working power, pulling out correct answers as fast as they can write them down on the page.

Isn't this a wonderful gift to give students, for only a few disciplined minutes each day, the final week before they take that test?

IN SUMMARY ....

A truly effective review is a continuous self-examination of the essential parts of a course.

This continuous self-examination goes on every week of the course, right up until the final examination. It takes place in three stages:

1. *The weekly review.* Where the child ties in every new chapter learned during the week with all the material that has gone before it. In this way students gain a constantly growing overall view of the course, with all its important parts fresh in mind.
2. *The final organization of the notebook.* Where they organize and blend in all the information they have received during the course—from the textbook, the lectures, the outside reference work, the vocabulary building, and the error feedback. From this blending, they gain a final unified outline of the backbone ideas of the course, all at their fingertips for instant reference.
3. *The final quiz-review of the entire course.* Where they write their own final exam on the important ideas they have learned in the entire term, becoming familiar and at ease with both the content and form of such an exam. From this final self-quiz, they gain dozens of the actual questions that will be asked in the final exam, plus the confidence that they can answer any other question that can be asked.

With this solid bedrock foundation of review to back them, we now turn to the final examinations themselves, and see dozens of simple ways to improve performance in them.

To the Student: Do It Yourself

To master a course, you must:

1. Find out what has to be learned in each course assignment.
2. Read that assignment to get at the heart of its meaning.
3. Write that core meaning down in your notebook, in a few brief sentences or phrases in outline form.
4. Tie the outline of that assignment into the assignment that came before it.
5. Review as much as you have studied of the entire book or course EVERY WEEK, to get an overall view.
6. At the end of the term, a week or two before the final test, make a final review of your strengths and weaknesses.

To review for a course, do NOT cram. Instead, practice these two essential steps:

1. Boil the material of the course down to its essentials, and then boil the essentials down again and again until you have mastered the core meaning.
2. Periodically review that core material—through continuous self-examinations—till every word of its content is ready to be instantly formed into an answer.

There are three steps to the process of review and readiness:

1. *The weekly review.* Where you tie in every new chapter learned during the week with all the material that has gone before it.
2. *The final organization of the notebook.* Where you organize and blend in all the information you have received—from the textbook, the lectures, the outside reference work, the vocabulary building, and the error feedback.
3. *The final quiz-review of the entire course.* Where you write your own final exam on the important ideas learned in the entire term, becoming familiar and at ease with both the content and form of such an exam.

How to Breeze Through Tests

THE WEEK BEFORE THE TEST

• • •

What to Do and What Not to Do

The final goal of all your child's planning—all the work, all the learning and relearning and review—is one or two or three hours in a closed room, proving the year's accomplishment, in the educational ritual called the *test,* which separates the winners from the losers.

Some parents object to tests as unfair, anxiety-causing, and not really proving anything. This is untrue. Life is a series of tests. Some are written, some are verbal, some are economic or social or moral.

In any case, your child had better get used to passing all of them now. The winner's circle is an entirely different world from the habitat of the also-ran.

The First Great Step in Improving Any Child's Test Grades

Test performance can be improved, just as performance in any competitive activity can be improved. And as in developing any other skill, the two magic ingredients are:

1. Knowledge   **Two Magic**
2. Practice   **Ingredients**

   And, as in any other form of payoff competition, there is always one great enemy to
face and overcome: fear.

Fear destroys students in tests, just as fear can   **Overcome Fear**
destroy their parents in later life. The student
who tenses up, panics, forgets all the carefully
stored information the moment it is necessary
to face the test paper, is beaten before even
trying.
   Therefore, the first step in preparing students to master any kind of examination is to
always ask this question:

What causes fear in a test situation?

The answer is twofold:

1. Not knowing the material upon which they   **Two Causes**
   are going to be tested.   **of Fear**
2. Not knowing the forms and procedures by
   which they will be tested.

   Either one of these two test fears can
knock students right out of a top grade. They
can cause a performance 30 percent to 50 percent *less* than students are really capable of
giving.
   You must prevent this loss. But how?

Quite simply, really, in these three tested and   **Three Steps to**
proved ways: **Prevent Loss**

1. Preparation
2. Familiarity
3. Practice

   Let's discuss each of them in turn:

Preparation

FIRST, of course, preparation. Knowing the material of the course. Knowing it backward and forward. Boiling it down into its main ideas; arranging those main ideas in the right logical order so that one automatically suggests another; and filing those ideas away in mind so permanently that they spring to the tongue or the hand the very instant they are needed.

This preparation for the final exam begins the very first day students enter class. This book has been a step-by-step blueprint on how to conduct that preparation, how to make it as thorough as possible, and how to make it instantly available again, at the moment of payoff.

Familiarity

SECOND, after students have mastered the content of the course, they must then equally master the forms by which they will be questioned about it.

Tests frighten students by their very appearance. The sight of a strange new way to ask a question can cause students to miss an answer that they know perfectly well. Questions, as all students know, can be tricky. *Your job is to take the trickery out of them before they are encountered in the test room.*

Demonstrate Questions

This demands that you sit down with your child and demonstrate, one by one, the types of questions that will be asked in the exams. You show how these questions are built, how to read them, what must be done to solve them, and how they themselves can help your child solve them.

Demonstrate Answers

Then you go over the same type of question two, three, four or more times, until your child is as familiar with the way to work out the answer to that question as with the way to write his or her own name.

Your goal is simple. You must make certain **Make Question**
that your child is never confronted with a type **Forms Familiar**
or form of question that has never been seen
before.

The moment students glance at that question, its form must be so familiar that they know automatically, without a second thought, the procedure by which they will answer it. They must be able to concentrate instantly on the content of that question, to devote full energies to retrieving the material that will answer it, without giving the form of the question a second thought.

This is what the next two chapters will do for your child. First, we will discuss every type of short-answer question now in popular use, then every type of essay question.

Our goal is to build into your child's test-taking personality, familiarity—the second great weapon against fear.

Practice

THIRD, and finally, once students know the course material, and once they know the form or type of questions they're going to be asked about it, then they put the two together in constant, continuous *practice.*

Students take tests from the very first day they open a book. *You* test them every single night in your parent Achievement Check. They test *themselves,* with every Main-Thought Outline they write each night, every tie-in talk they have each morning, every weekly review they finish each Friday.

Every time they do a problem in mathematics, they test themselves. Every time they correct an error in their homework, they retest themselves.

Every day, they subject themselves to a barrage of questions. Till questions become second nature to them. Till they can smell a possible test question on a printed page a mile away. *Till their minds become one great razor-sharp instrument for asking and answering questions. And, at that moment, you can take credit not only for top grades, but for having developed a truly educated child.*

Education is, in the last analysis, the ability to ask and answer questions. It is active knowledge seeking out new knowledge to deepen its understanding. It is thought in action, able to learn, to solve, to build. It is probably the most precious gift, after love, that you will ever hand on to your child.

The Study Schedule for the Final Two Weeks Before the Test

Fortunately, this continuous question-and-answer approach to education keeps students constantly reviewing, constantly prepared for whatever tests they may encounter. Therefore, as we have seen in the previous chapter, the formal preparation for their final test requires much less time than that needed by their less organized classmates.

Once again, however, for these final two weeks, they draw up a definite plan of attack. To get the greatest benefit out of every study hour, for every course, they do this:

Get the Greatest Benefit Out of Every Study Hour

1. They divide the last two weeks before the final test into six working days. They then decide how many hours they will have in each working day to devote to study—let us say three hours a day. This gives eighteen working hours per week for the last two weeks.
2. They then take the number of courses they will have to study for. Let us say there are four. Thus, four courses into eighteen hours each week gives four hours plus during the week to devote to each course.

   If one course is slightly harder than the

others, they devote an extra hour or two to it. But in any case they set up a definite allotment of study hours for each of the courses before beginning the final review for them.

3. During the first week, the review will consist of rewriting and blending notes, as detailed in Chapter 21. Let us assume they spend all the allotted four hours per course in that first week on this active rewriting of the notes.

4. During the final week, they devote the first two hours to taking those notes and writing their own final exam about them.

They then devote the third hour—a day later—to taking this self-exam, checking the weak points, reviewing the material that will deepen their understanding of them, and marking each still-troublesome idea for one last review the next day.

The Final Hour of Preparation— Preferably with a Friend

They are now ready for the last self-exam. They will take it on this basis:

What your child has done up to this point has been a process of condensation, of boiling down the material of each course in two ways:

- First, to its main thoughts, its backbone meaning, its important ideas that he or she must be tested upon.
- Second, to each one of those main ideas that is particularly hard, that he or she does not quite understand, that cannot be answered as quickly and accurately as all the others.

Throughout the hours and hours of self-examination, your child has gradually mastered and put aside those important ideas that he or she thoroughly understands. In the two weeks of final review, your child first refreshed his or her memory on these well-known facts, and then tested the ability to recall them easily and completely.

Now they have been put aside. Your child *knows* that he or she can answer any test question about them.

This leaves your child, in this last hour of review, face to face with his or her own particular troublemakers.

These are the facts upon which your child is vague. The problems that cannot be solved automatically. The questions that might trip him or her up without this one final hour of mastery.

Now your child attacks them directly, in every form, shape, and way that can be thought of.

If possible, *you* should be with your child in this final hour of mastery. Your job here is that of question asker. You should take every one of those troublemakers in turn, and invent five, six, seven different approaches, different questions to sharpen your child's mind about them.

For example, take the first of them, and first ask a true-false question about it. Then switch to a multiple-answer question. Then to a cross-out question. Then to a comparison-contrast question.

Ask as many questions as you can think up about that one troublemaker. Keep asking till the right answer becomes automatic on your child's lips. Then go on to the next troublemaker and do the same.

Of course, familiarity with the subject matter will greatly aid this final, intensive quiz. Therefore, for at least this last hour, it is advisable that your child review this material with another serious friend.

Let us assume that both students have prepared for their final exams in approximately the same way described above. In this case, both have prepared their own self-quiz on the same material.

But no two minds think alike, and one may have picked some vital point that the other has neglected. Therefore, for the first half-hour of this last review hour, have them give each other their own quizzes.

This should be done orally. Fast. With the answers springing from their lips almost the instant the questions are finished.

Many of the questions your child will have already anticipated, almost phrased exactly the same. Realizing this will give each child's confidence a huge boost.

Other questions will be slight rephrases, or on different points that the students might have stressed. This will give both a chance to pull the material out of their mind, to become accustomed to turning questions into answers automatically.

When the quizzes are over, both students turn to their trouble-makers. They intensively quiz each other on just these points. They discuss their answers. The two points of view merge. New insights are gained by each. This may be the final push that leads your child to absolute understanding of a point that has been bothering him or her since the beginning of the school year, so your child can now file it away and forget it.

How to Make Sure Your Child Remembers Memory Work When Going into the Examination Room

In addition to this backbone meaning of the course, your child will be confronted from time to time with other facts, equally important, which must be memorized exactly, detail for detail. These may be mathematical formulas, history dates, equations in chemistry or physics, and so on.

With such facts, the problem is one of sheer memorization. They must be engraved on the memory by the time your child walks into the examination room. Students can do this most easily by using flash cards:

1. They buy a packet of 5 1/2 by 8 inch index cards that fit into their pocket. Each formula they want to memorize, they write down exactly on one of these cards. They use a separate card for each formula they wish to retain.

2. On the front of each card they write down the name of the for-mula. For example, they might write on the front of one card:

To find the area of a circle.

3. On the back of the card, they write the formula itself:

    $A = \pi R^2$

4. They carry these cards with them to every class. Whenever they have a spare moment, they pull them out, look at the identifying name on the front, and try to recite the exact formula from memory. They then turn the card over to see if they are correct.

5. When they have repeated the correct formula three times from memory, they take the card and file it away till the week before the final test. If they cannot repeat it three times from memory, they continue in this way:

6. The final week before the test, each night they take the difficult formulas and lay them in a pile face up on the study table. They read the names one by one and write down the formulas on a piece of paper. Then they check their answers against the backs of the cards.

7. Right or wrong, they continue this writing and checking procedure for five nights before the final test.

8. On the day of the test, in the morning before they leave for school, they run through the hardest of the cards again—writing and then checking and, if necessary, correcting.

9. They then take these hard-formula cards to school. When they reach the test room, one minute before the test begins, they take out the cards again. They take them one by one, and this time they write the formula down on the face of the card, underneath the name.

10. They then check the back of the card to see if they are right. If they are right, they underline the correct formula on the front of the card. If they are wrong, they write down the correct formula on the front of the card once more.

11. Then they tear up the cards and throw them away. They walk directly to their desks, take the exam paper as soon as it is given, and write the correct formulas in its margin.

They now have the correct formulas at their fingertips, ready to go to work for them in the examination.

The Night Before the Test

One last note on this final week before the test. We have tried to prepare your child as perfectly as humanly possible for this examination. We therefore assume that he or she is ready to take this final exam—as only one of a series of examinations given all year long—the day before the test.

Therefore, any final study the night before the test would only be wasted effort. Let your child relax that night. A good dinner, perhaps an early movie or soda with the family, then a sound night's sleep.

Your child will forget nothing in that final night's relaxation. He or she is prepared and can take the test the next morning with absolute self-confidence.

 **IN SUMMARY** ....

There are three simple secrets to achieving the absolute top grades in any test your child will ever take:

1. Preparation—to master the content of the course.
2. Familiarity—with the types of questions that will be asked.
3. Practice—to combine this content and form into a flawless routine of instant-precision answers.

After a final week of such practice, your child should be able to walk into the examination room with complete self-assurance.

To help your child do this, we now examine the type of questions that will be asked, and how any pitfalls they may present can be avoided.

To the Student: Do It Yourself

- You must have knowledge of the subject, and you must practice.
- You must also overcome the enemy—fear.
- You must know the material on which you will be tested and know the procedures by which you will be tested:

Preparation / Familiarity / Practice

- Review and practice questions you might be asked.
- Two weeks before any test, figure out how many hours you have each day to study for each course. Some courses may need more time than others.
- During the first week, blend and rewrite your notes from the course.
- Write down all the important ideas. Put aside the ones you fully understand.
- Make a separate list of those ideas that give you trouble.
- Ask yourself as many possible questions about these ideas as you can think of—in every possible way: multiple-choice, true-false, cross-out, compare-contrast, etc., until you are sure of this material.
- Go over this material with a friend who has prepared his or her own questions. Then you each answer the other's questions, reviewing the answers together.
- During the final week, write a practice final exam based upon your notes.
- The next day, take the practice exam. Review your answers. Go over your weak points until they are second nature to you.
- When you have formulas, dates, equations, etc., you must memorize them. Write them down on index cards, putting the question on one side and the answer on the other. Carry them around and study them at any free moment.
- As you learn each fact, file the card away. The week before the test, take them out and review them again.

CHAPTER

TYPES OF SHORT-
ANSWER TESTS

• • •

How to Master Them

The most frequent type of test students will encounter is the objective or short-answer or write-in test.

Such tests—and there are at least ten different forms of them—present a series of short questions to students, and then ask them to give a short answer to each. Often this answer is no more than a single word, a yes or a no, or a check mark in the proper space.

Thus these short-answer tests require no writing skill on the part of students. During an entire test, they may not write a single sentence.

Because of this, many parents falsely believe that these write-in tests are nothing but measurements of memory, that they do not require their children to think, and that the child with the strongest memory is the child who will score highest on such tests.

Nothing could be further from the truth. A working knowledge of the facts—memorization—is only the first step required to score top marks on such short-answer tests. Assuming that students are thoroughly prepared in the content of their course—as we have tried to achieve in this book—they must also bring to the test at least three other vital skills.

The Three Skills Students Must Master to Get Top Grades on Objective Tests

If students want to get top grades on objective tests, they absolutely must master three skills.

1. They must learn to read with precision.
2. They must learn to make judgments between right and wrong choices.
3. They must learn to reason a problem, step by step, to its conclusion.

In this section I will show parents and students just what skills must be mastered to excel on objective tests.

1. Learn to Read with Precision

Short-answer tests are tricky tests. They are designed to expose the sloppy thinker and the careless reader. Time after time, their most heavily graded questions will turn on a single key word.

For example, take this true-false question in American history:

TRUE OR FALSE: **EXAMPLE**
Many pioneers died in Death Valley where the
climate is hot and humid.

This statement is perfectly true right up until the last word, which is false, and which therefore turns the entire statement false.

Therefore, students must be able to pick out those key words at a glance, understand whether they ask a straight or twisted question, and thus avoid the traps that destroy unwary classmates.

2. Learn to Make Judgments Between Right and Wrong Choices

Most short-answer tests do not merely ask for the right answer to a question; instead they furnish students with a series of possible answers—both right and wrong—to that question.

For example, take this typical question from an English vocabulary test:

Choose the answer which is most nearly OPPOSITE **EXAMPLE**
in meaning to the word in capital letters.

1. UNFIT:
   (A) tight
   (B) qualified
   (C) chosen
   (D) serene
   (E) necessary

With such a question, it is equally as important to be able to eliminate the wrong answers (tight, chosen, serene, necessary) as it is to be able to select qualified as the right answer.

This calls for *test judgment.* In a moment, we'll show you how students can develop it.

3. Learn to Reason a Problem, Step by Step, to Its Conclusion

And always, of course, in every test, on every question, students must be able to think. To work from the facts that are given to the facts that are asked for.

For example, take this problem from a College Entrance Exam:

Fill in the next two numbers in the following **EXAMPLE**
progression:
5, 9, 13, 17, 21, 25, 29, ___, ___,

Here students must be able to find a pattern (that each number is 4 higher than the number before it), and project that pattern to come up with the correct answers, 33 and 37.

And they must be able to set up these reasoning patterns, and put them to use, almost as fast as they can run their eyes over the question. We'll show you how in a moment.

So there you have them. The three *test abilities* **The Three Test**
students must bring to every examination: **Abilities Students Must Bring to Every Examination**

1. The ability to read with precision.
2. The ability to make judgments between right and wrong choices.
3. The ability to reason through a problem.

Now, let's see how we can sharpen each one of those abilities in your child.

Let's turn to the *ten* most common types of short-answer questions and examine them one by one.

Let's see how some of these questions demand emphasis on one ability, and other questions require another.

And let's learn the simple techniques that *double* the power of your child's abilities on each one of these questions, whenever they are encountered on a test.

Short-Answer Question Type 1: *True-False*

The true-false question is the simplest form of short-answer question. It presents a statement to students, and asks them to tell whether they consider that statement true or false.

Definition

There are several forms of the true-false question. They look like this:

What They Look Like

A. Write-In Form

George Washington was the first president of the United States. _____

Here the word *true* or *false* is to be written in after the statement.

B. Circle Form

T   F   George Washington was the first president of the United States.

Here students circle the T or F, or underline one, or check one, or in some other positive way mark their choice.

C. Cross-Out Form

Here the question looks the same as the circle form shown above:

T   F   George Washington was the first president of the United States.

However, in this test, the *instructions* for the test indicate that students should *cross out* the *wrong* choice, rather than mark the right choice. Here, for example, they would *cross out* the F, rather than underline the T.

It is *essential* that students read the instructions thoroughly at the beginning of *every* test, to avoid any confusion between these two types of true-false choices. A single overlooked word here can lead to costly and unnecessary mistakes.

D. Separate Answer-Sheet Form

Here the question is written on one paper and space for the answer is on a separate answer sheet, which is usually graded by a machine.

Each question and answer set is, of course, numbered, and looks like this:

On the question sheet:

17. George Washington was the first president of the United States.

On the answer sheet:

17. T   F
    [] []

With such a test, neatness and precision again become crucial. It is incredible how many students lose grades on such tests, simply because they place the right answer in the wrong space. It is your job to make sure that such waste can never happen with your child.

How to Master True-False Questions

A true-false question is either completely right or it's wrong. In other words, every single word in the question must be utterly true, or the entire question is false. If there is one exception to the statement, it's false.

Therefore, every word counts. One tiny word, **Every Word** anywhere in the statement, can turn it from **Counts** true to false. Here, precision reading pays off.

Students should underline the key words of each statement in this way:

Harry S. Truman, born in _Independence,_ Missouri, was _33rd_ president of the United States.

Here are two key facts that must be true to make the statement true. Truman must have been born in _Independence_, not in Saint Louis or Kansas City. And he must have been the _33rd_ president of the United States, not the 32nd or 34th.

Since the first fact is false—President Truman was _not_ born in Independence—the whole statement is false.

The procedure for answering a true-false question, therefore, is this:

The Procedure for Answering a True-False Question

1. Read the statement carefully.
2. Read it again, underlining the key words.
3. Determine whether each key word, each key fact, is true or false.
4. If any key fact is wrong, the statement is wrong. Only if all the key facts are correct can the statement be true.

In a true-false test students should always be suspicious of flat statements that allow no exceptions. They are probably false. Tip-offs include such words as:

What to Watch Out For

- All
- Always
- Absolutely
- Any
- Every
- Invariably
- No
- Never
- None

When students see such a word in a true-false question, they should automatically mark it false unless they are absolutely sure that there is no exception to its rule.

On the other hand, the following moderate words in a true-false question are usually tip-offs that the question is true:

- Many
- Often
- On the average
- Some
- Usually

When they encounter such words, students should mark the question true, unless they find a key fact later in the statement that twists it false.

Short-Answer Question Type 2: *Multiple Choice*

The multiple-choice test lists a number of possible answers after each of its questions. One of these answers is right; the rest are wrong. It is your child's task to choose the correct one.

Definition

The multiple-choice question may list its answers on the same line as the question itself, like this:

What Multiple-Choice Looks Like

1. American fighter planes are usually armed with machine guns of .22 .30 .32 .45 .50 .57 caliber.

EXAMPLE 1

Or it may list the answers on separate lines, like this:

2. An efficient student—
   a. Studies with the radio volume lowered.
   b. Studies at least two hours for every hour spent in class each week.

EXAMPLE 2

    c. Does most reviewing just prior to an exami-
       nation.
    d. Does not make notations in the textbook.

It may list the answers as part of an incomplete statement, as in the examples above. Or it may ask a complete question, with separate answers listed below it, like this:

3.   Which of the following is not an effective   **EXAMPLE 3**
    study habit?
    a. Studying in the same place each day.
    b. Revising notes immediately after lectures.
    c. Having a separate notebook for each class.

How to Master Multiple-Choice Questions

Whatever its form, the multiple-choice question forces students to choose and reject. And it does not make this choice easy. In fact, it often deliberately confuses, by furnishing answers that are designed to look *near-correct,* and thus throw students off the track.

For example, take this question from a vocabulary test. It asks students to choose the definition that is nearest in meaning to the first capitalized word.

4.   IMPOSTURE—   **EXAMPLE 4**
    a. excessive burden
    b. stooping position
    c. fraud
    d. handicap

In this case, the correct answer is **c. fraud.** But there are two deliberately misleading choices designed to draw students away from that correct answer, if they do not know it thoroughly.

The first is **a. excessive burden,** which is a definition of IMPOSITION, a word similar to imposture.

The second is **b. stooping position,** which plays on a possible misreading by students of the -POSTURE part of the question word. Because of these built-in traps, a definite step-by-step technique is essential in answering multiple-choice questions. Let's examine that technique, right now:

Step-by-Step Technique for Answering Multiple-Choice Questions

Step One: Anticipate the Answer

In multiple-choice questions like Examples 1 and 4 above, where the question or incomplete-statement part makes sense by itself alone, without students reading on to the list of possible answers, train them to do this:

First, read the first part of the question (For example, in Example 4 they read just the word IMPOSTURE) and then stop.

First, Read the First Part of the Question

Second, before they go to the list of possible answers, have them lightly jot down on the side of the paper what they believe is the correct answer.

Second, Jot Down a Possible Answer

For example, they may immediately realize that IMPOSTURE means fakery or fraud. Or they associate it with IMPOSTOR, a person who is a fraud. Let them lightly sketch the idea of fraud next to the answer, and then go on with the next step.

Third, they then look for what they believe is the correct answer among the list of possible answers printed on the test.

Finally, Look for the Correct Answer

For example, when they see **c. fraud** in the list of answers, they can be almost certain that they have it right.

So the procedure in Step One—anticipating the answer—is first to read the question part of the statement, then jot down what they think is the correct answer, then look for that correct answer in the list of possible answers that completes the question.

Summary of Step One

Now, in Examples 2 and 3 above, this technique must be altered slightly. Here the question part does not make sense by itself (for example, in 2, it says only: *"An efficient student—"*)

Therefore they must read on, over each of the possible answers, *making a light pencil check mark on the answer they believe is correct as soon as they read it.* For example, they read on to:

> a. Studies with the radio volume lowered.   **From EXAMPLE 2**

They do not believe this is correct. So they go on to:

> b. Studies at least two hours for every hour spent in class.

This they believe is correct. So they check it lightly and go on to the second step.

Step Two: Read Every Possible Answer

Now, once students have anticipated what they believe is the correct answer, they must make absolutely sure that they are right. They do this by a process of checking and elimination.

To begin this check, they now read every possible answer on the list. For example, in Example 2 above, they go on to read:

> c. Does most reviewing just prior to an exami-   **From EXAMPLE 2**
>   nation.

And they also read:

> d. Does not make notations in the textbook.

Step Three: Eliminate the Wrong Answers

Now, as they read each of these other possible answers, they eliminate them one by one as being incorrect. Only when they have rejected all other answers except the correct one—only when they have proved that they are wrong—can they be certain that their choice is absolutely right.

To do this, they must give a reason why each rejected answer is wrong. Let's see how they do this in Example 2 above:

They read:

   a. Studies with the radio volume lowered.   **From EXAMPLE 2**

They immediately reject this answer as wrong, because the good student does not have the radio on when studying at all. They then read:

   c. Does most of the reviewing just prior to an examination.

Which is wrong because review is a continuous process, starting the first day of study. And then they finish the list by reading:

   d. Does not make notations in the textbook.

Which is again wrong because the good student will underline in the textbook the essence of each chapter before transferring that essence to the notebook.

They have now cross-checked the answer. They have anticipated the one correct answer; they have read all the others; and they have rejected them as wrong. They are now sure they are right.

Step Four: Mark Down the Correct Answer

They then mark down this correct answer, and go on to the next question.

How the Question or the Choices Sometimes Help You Find the Correct Answer

If students are well prepared, the technique outlined above will make them absolutely certain that they have the correct answer to over 90 percent of all multiple-choice questions.

However, there will always be a question or two in every test where students are not sure of the correct answer. They may be confused; they may have temporarily forgotten it; they may need just a slight nudge to regain it again.

In this case, the question itself may help them clear up this confusion and point the way to the correct answer. Let's examine some of the techniques by which they can use the structure or makeup of that question to help find the correct answer.

Eliminate the Wrong Answers First

In most multiple-choice questions, students may not be sure which of the possible answers is correct, but they probably can tell that some of them are definitely wrong. In this case, since it is easier to choose among two answers than five, they should immediately cross out the answers that they know are wrong.

For example, in Example 4 they may be confused between whether IMPOSTURE is **a. an excessive burden** or **c. a fraud.** But they are sure that it is not **b. a stooping position** or **d. a handicap.** So they eliminate these two possibilities, and thus focus their attention on the two remaining possibilities, to which they now apply the following techniques.

Rephrase the Question

Often the memory prod students need to come up with the right answer can be furnished by rephrasing the question. By turning a positive question into a negative one, by turning a noun asked for into a verb, or any other way of gaining a new slant on the question.

For example, in Example 4 instead of wrestling with IMPOSTURE, the act of defrauding, students may try changing the word into IMPOSTOR, a person who defrauds. Here they have a word that is far more familiar to them, and that immediately clears up any question they might have had about whether the word could mean an excessive burden.

In the same way, in Example 3, if they were torn between answers b and c, students would rephrase the question in this way:

> Which of the following IS an effective study   **From EXAMPLE 3**
> habit?
> b. Revising notes immediately after class? *YES.*
> c. Having a separate notebook for each class?
>   *NO.*

The answer becomes obvious immediately. By simply stating the OPPOSITE to the original question asked, the correct answer is thrown into clear focus.

Try to Eliminate Extremes

Some multiple-choice questions, such as Example 1 will have a scale of answers. This question asks students to complete the statement:

American fighter planes are usually armed with **From EXAMPLE 1** machine guns of .22 .30 .32 .45 .50 .57 caliber.

On scale questions like this one, if they are not certain of the correct answer at once, students should start to work on the question by trying to eliminate the .22 and .57 caliber extremes. In most cases, these will be incorrect, and will leave only four possible answers to choose from, rather than six.

Look for Internal Clues

Many multiple-choice questions help students answer them, simply because of their own construction. In some cases this construction eliminates certain possible answers; in others it points almost directly to the correct answer. Let us look at an example of each.

Which of the following were, in part, results of   **EXAMPLE**
the immigration policy of the United States during the latter half of the nineteenth century?
1. Supply of cheap labor.
2. Growth of urban populations.
3. Opposition of organized labor to immigration
     policy.
4. Decline in birth rate.

(A) 1 and 2 only.
(B) 1 and 3 only.
(C) 1, 2 and 3 only.
(D) 1, 2 and 4 only.
(E) 1, 2, 3 and 4.

Use the Test-Furnished Clue

Notice that all five possible answers above include result 1—supply of cheap labor. Therefore, instantly, students can assume that this answer is correct, and use it as a test-furnished clue to help choose the correct answer from the other choices.

In this case, of course, the fact that the immigration policy increased the supply of labor also meant that it increased the growth of urban populations, and that it naturally produced an opposition of organized labor to this incoming cheap labor supply. It did not, however, decrease in any way the birth rate, but probably raised it.

Therefore, by using the first possible correct answer as a clue, and logically applying its information to the remaining answers, students pulled out the final answer, even though they did not know that answer when they first read the question.

The same technique of making the question furnish its own answer applies in the following example:

The action of *A Tale of Two Cities* takes place in: **EXAMPLE**
1. Glasgow and London
2. New York and Paris
3. Vienna and Rome
4. Paris and London
5. Dublin and Edinburgh

Here students simply notice that only two cities are mentioned twice in the list of possible answers—**Paris** and **London.** Since these cities are mentioned twice—once together and once each with a third city to catch the unwary or careless student—it's highly probable that they are the correct answers. Which they are.

Look for Signs of Extra Care

Finally, if they are stumped on a multiple-choice question, students should always check to see if one of the possible answers is longer, or in a different vocabulary, or in any other way has had extra care spent on it, more than the other answers in the list. If it has, this is a definite clue that it might be the correct answer.

For example, take this question from a College   **EXAMPLE**
Board test on chemistry:

The burning of gasoline in an automobile involves all of the following EXCEPT
(A) reduction
(B) decomposition
(C) an exothermic reaction

(D) oxidation
(E) conversion of matter to energy

Here two separate signs of extra care coincide to point out answer **(E)** as the correct one.

How to Spot Signs of Extra Care

- First, it is much longer than the other answers.
- Second, it uses a different vocabulary— talking in plain English rather than technical terms.

These two clues should lead students to strongly suspect that answer **(E)** is the one they are looking for. Which it is.

Of course, all these techniques of making the question help students answer it are merely supplements to their own preparation and knowledge. Ideally, they should be used merely to help them check the fact that they know the right answer, or as memory prods to help them over a temporary block in retrieving that answer from their storehouse of knowledge. They are never substitutes for study or ability.

A Note on the Mastery of Multiple-Choice Questions in Vocabulary Tests

Most vocabulary tests—and they are extremely important to students' progress in both their schoolwork and on intelligence tests— are phrased in the form of multiple-choice questions.

These questions will ask for either synonyms (words that mean the same as the given word) or antonyms (words that mean the opposite of the given word). A synonym question is given in Example 4 above. An antonym question, from an earlier example, is repeated below.

Choose the answer which is most nearly OPPOSITE in meaning to the word in capital letters.

EXAMPLE

1. UNFIT:
   (A) tight
   (B) qualified

(C) chosen
(D) serene
(E) necessary

Such an antonym question is really two questions in one, and deserves a special technique of its own to solve it. Here it is:

Step One: **Think of a Synonym for the Word**

The moment students read the capitalized word, they should stop without reading on. *Before* they look at the list of possible answers, they should jot down a synonym. For example, in this case, they might think of *not fit, incapable, unqualified.*

Step Two: **Think of the Opposite of That Synonym**

Now—again *before* they read the list of possible answers—students jot down the *opposite* of the synonym on their paper. They write *fit, capable, qualified.*

Step Three: **Read the Answer List, Eliminate, and Choose**

They now read each possible answer in turn, comparing it with their own ideas. They reject **tight;** are delighted to find the exact word they had anticipated, **qualified,** as the second possible answer; then go on to eliminate **chosen, serene,** and **necessary** as a final check.

In this step-by-step way, such problems become simple, and confusion and trickery are both side-stepped.

One more clue to help students solve these vocabulary tests. The word they are looking for in the answer list should be the same grammatical term as the given, capitalized word. **Look for Similar Part of Speech**

If the given word is a noun, the correct answer should be a noun. If the given word is a verb, the correct answer should be a verb. And so on.

If, on the other hand, one of the possible answers is a different grammatical term (for instance, a verb when the given word is a noun), then it should be automatically eliminated as incorrect.

Short-Answer Question Type 3: *Completion*

A completion question is similar to a multiple-choice question. But instead of choosing the correct answer from a list of perhaps five possibilities, students must provide the answer themselves, writing it in the blank space provided on the test form.

Definition of a Completion Question

A completion question that asked for the same information as Example 1 above would look like this:

American fighter planes are usually armed with machine guns of_____ caliber.

EXAMPLE

How to Master Completion Questions

A completion question demands knowledge and preparation. Students must know the answer when they walk into the test room. The only clues that will be given—and these are very slight—are the following:

1. Look for the Number of Blanks

The number of blanks that are furnished. For example, in this question:

In the lungs the blood exchanges _____ _____ for oxygen.

EXAMPLE

The two blank spaces indicate that two words will make up the correct answer. This may give students the hint they need to retrieve *carbon dioxide* from their memory storehouse.

2. Look for an Article

A or *an* in front of the blank space. For example, in this question:

A bird that can't fly is called an _____. **EXAMPLE**

The *an* clue may lead students to rule out *kiwi* and come up with *ostrich* as the correct answer.

3. Look for a Verb

A verb clue as to single or plural answers.

None of these clues, however, is, as with any other type of question, a substitute for sheer hard preparation.

Short-Answer Question Type 4: *Enumeration*

An enumeration question asks students to list a number of series of facts. It does not require the list to be given in any set order. It usually begins with the words *list* or *name*.

Definition

For example:

List the members of the President's cabinet.

What Enumeration Questions Looks Like

How to Master Enumeration Questions

Here again, preparation is critical. If you know that your child and the other students will be given enumeration questions on their tests, help prepare for them by:

1. Giving such questions on the review self-examinations. And make sure that all the items in the series are gotten down on the paper.

2. In a series-enumeration question, have the items in the series numbered. Thus, if your child knows that there are fourteen members of the President's cabinet, he or she will not list only thirteen on the exam paper by mistake, and forget to put in the fourteenth.

Short-Answer Question Type 5: *Sequence*

A sequence question asks students to list a series of facts in their proper order. Usually this will be the order in which historical events happened.

Definition

Or, as a combination of the sequence and multiple-choice type of questions, students may be supplied with a list of events and asked to number them according to time.

The first form would be as simple as this:

What Sequence Questions Look Like

List the first five Presidents of the United States in the order that they held office.

The second form would look like this:

Number the following events in order of sequence:
___ Congress of Berlin
___ Monroe Doctrine
___ Boxer Rebellion
___ Mexican War

How to Master Sequence Questions

In dealing with the second form, there are two tactics to follow:

1. Look for the first and last items of the series and number them first. Then look for the second and next-to-last items. And so on. In this way, students are again getting

Get Rid of the Extremes First

rid of the extremes first. And in this way narrowing down the area of choice and possibilities of making a mistake.

2. Number those items of which you are sure first. With a long list, your child should take a piece of scratch paper and re-create the list on it, putting down the items of which he or she is sure in their proper positions, and then simply using the other items to fill in the gaps.

Short-Answer Question Type 6: *Matching*

A matching question usually consists of two lists of items placed side by side. Students are asked to match the items on one list with the items on the other by marking the letters from the first list in the spaces provided in front of the second.

Definition

Write the letter of each of the cities in front of the state of which it is the capital.

What Matching Questions Look Like

A. Frankfort   ___ South Dakota
B. Pierre   ___ Kentucky
C. Omaha   ___ California
D. Sacramento   ___ Nevada
E. Carson City   ___ Nebraska

How to Master Matching Questions

Again, elimination of known answers is the key. There are two quick methods of doing this:

1. Students should run light pencil lines between those items on the first and second lists that they are absolutely sure of.
2. Have them cross off an item in the second list as soon as they mark its letter on the first list.

In this way they eliminate the sure answers first and are able to concentrate attention on the one or two remaining items that need more thought without being confused.

Here again, they must remember that *tests also teach*. They give information as well as demand it. Many clues are contained in a matching question that will help pull out the correct answer.

Remember That Tests Also Teach

For example, in the question above, they may not know that Carson City is the capital of Nevada, but may know that it is a city in that state. The mere fact that it is mentioned in a list of state capitals then tells all that is needed to know the question correctly.

Short-Answer Question Type 7: *Cross Out*

A cross-out question is one that asks your child to eliminate the wrong item in a series.

Definition

For example:

Cross out the numbers that do not belong in the following series:

5 10 20 40 50 60 80 160 320

What Cross-Out Questions Look Like

How to Master Cross-Out Questions

Cross-out questions are difficult for most students because they are really two-part questions and must be done one part at a time. If your child tries to do both parts at the same time, or just plunges hopelessly into the question without an organized technique, he or she will become immediately lost.

With technique, however, the cross-out question is really quite simple. Here is the proper procedure:

Step One: Define What Is Happening in the Series

The first thing students must do when they encounter a series of numbers is to find out what is going on in that series. Are the numbers increasing or decreasing? Is another number being added to them or subtracted from them? If so, how big is that number? Or are they doubling, or tripling, or halving? What is the principle that determines what the next number will be?

In this way they eliminate the sure answers first and are able to concentrate attention on the one or two remaining items that need more prodding without being confused.

For example, in the series above, students start by asking, "What happens to 5 that makes it 10?" There are two answers: Either 5 more is added to it, or it is doubled.

They next go on to the relation between 10 and 20. They ask themselves, "What happens to 10 that makes it 20?" Again there are two possible answers: Either 10 more is added to it, or it is doubled.

Now they have a pattern. The number 5 was doubled to make 10, and 10 was doubled to make 20. They now believe that they know what is going on in the series: each number is doubled to make the next.

They now test this pattern on the next number. It is 40. The number 20 is doubled to make 40, so it fits. The pattern still holds.

If the pattern is correct, the next number should be 80. But it's 50 instead. So they go on to:

Step Two: Locate the Wrong Items and Cross Them Out

The number 50 does not follow the double pattern, so they put a light line through it—to indicate that they believe for the moment it should be crossed out—and go on to the next number.

This number is 60. Again, it doesn't fit the double pattern. And again they put a light line through it and go on to the next number.

This number is 80. Here the pattern takes over again. They have expected 80, and found it. This indicates that both 50 and 60 were wrong numbers and should be crossed out.

But, to make certain, they still have two remaining numbers to check out the pattern. They now test each of them.

The next number is 160. The number 80 doubled is 160. The pattern fits.

The next number is 320. The number 160 doubled is 320. Again the pattern fits.

They are now certain that 50 and 60 are the wrong numbers. They cross them out and go on to the next question.

This same two-part technique will be used to solve the "terror of the classrooms," which is:

Short-Answer Question Type 8: *Number Series*

The number-series question presents students with a series of numbers again, but this time all are correct, and they are required to write down the next one or two numbers at the end of the series.

Definition

A number-series question is usually presented in groups, starting with easy ones and ending up with the very difficult. Here is a sample you might find on any college admission test:

What Number-Series Questions Look Like

1. 5 9 13 17 21 25 29 ___ ___

2. 40 30 20 10 ___

3. 6 18 54 162 486 ___ ___

4. 7 10 14 15 18 22 23 ___

5. 3 7 5 9 7 11 9 ___ ___

6. 12 8 9 14 6 20 3 ___

7. 2 4 8 3 9 27 4 ___ ___

Again, every number-series question is a two-part question. Its first part must be solved first before students can begin to answer it finally.

How to Master Number-Series Questions

Here are the two questions they must answer before they can solve any number-series question:

1. What is happening in this series? What kind of progression is going on?
2. What, then, must the next one or two numbers in this series be?

The first question must be answered correctly before they can answer the second. Therefore your son's or daughter's first job in attacking any number-series question is to *discover and mark down the series pattern.*

In fact, it is so important that they thoroughly understand this pattern that they actually mark it down on the test paper like this:

SERIES 1: 5 9 13 17 21 25 29___ ___

In Series 1 above, they ask themselves, "What happens to 5 that makes it 9?" The answer is that 4 is added to it, and they draw a line between the 5 and the 9 and mark down +4 on top of that line, like this:

$$\overset{+4}{\overline{5\ \ 9}}$$

Now they ask, "What happens to 9 that makes it 13?" The answer is again plus 4. And they again draw a line between the two numbers and mark +4 above it like this:

$$\overset{+4}{\overline{5}}\ \overset{+4}{\overline{9\ \ 13}}$$

A physical, concrete pattern that *they can see* is now beginning to emerge before their eyes. They continue this marking of the pattern through every number in the series, until, when they have finished the first step, the question now looks like this:

$$\overset{+4}{\overline{5}}\ \overset{+4}{\overline{9}}\ \overset{+4}{\overline{13}}\ \overset{+4}{\overline{17}}\ \overset{+4}{\overline{21}}\ \overset{+4}{\overline{25}}\ \overline{29}\ \_\_\ \_\_$$

The pattern is now obvious. To answer the second part of the question, they simply add 4 to 29 to get 33, and then add 4 again to get 37.

SERIES 2: 40 30 20 10 ___

This same technique of marking the pattern greatly simplifies all number-series questions. In Series 2, for instance, the pattern –10 emerges, and the problem looks like this:

$$\overbrace{40}^{} \overbrace{30}^{-10} \overbrace{20}^{-10} \overbrace{10}^{-10} \underline{}$$

At this point, the answer quite obviously becomes 0.

SERIES 3: 6 18 54 162 486 ___ ___

In Series 3, the pattern ×3 emerges, and the problem looks like this:

$$\overbrace{6 \quad 18}^{\times3} \overbrace{54}^{\times3} \overbrace{162}^{\times3} \overbrace{486}^{\times3} \underline{} \underline{}$$

The answers thus become 1,458 and 4,374.

SERIES 4: 7 10 14 15 18 22 23 ___ ___

In Series 4, the pattern becomes more complicated. In Series 1, 2, and 3, the same pattern held for every number in the series. In Series 1, the pattern +4 held for every number. In Series 2, the pattern –10 held for every number. And in Series 3, the pattern ×3 held for every number.

But in Series 4, no one pattern holds throughout the series. The pattern between the first two numbers looks like this:

$$\overbrace{7 \quad 10}^{+3}$$

The pattern between the second and third numbers emerges like this:

$$\overbrace{7 \quad 10}^{+3} \overbrace{14}^{+4}$$

And the pattern between the third and fourth numbers looks like this:

$$\overset{+3}{}\ \overset{+4}{}\ \overset{+1}{}$$
$$7 \quad 10 \quad 14 \quad 15$$

So far there is no relation between these two-number patterns. But in the next two numbers, this pattern emerges:

$$\overset{+3}{}\ \overset{+4}{}\ \overset{+1}{}\ \overset{+3}{}$$
$$7 \quad 10 \quad 14 \quad 15 \quad 18$$

The +3 pattern has repeated itself. Is this a coincidence, or is it the beginning of a new cycle of a +3+4+1 pattern? To find out, students test the next two numbers. If it is a new cycle, the next pattern should be +4, and the next number should be 22:

$$\overset{+3}{}\ \overset{+4}{}\ \overset{+1}{}\ \overset{+3}{}\ \overset{+4}{}$$
$$7 \quad 10 \quad 14 \quad 15 \quad 18 \quad 22$$

It is, of course. And the final number should then be 23, to give this final look to the problem:

$$\overset{+3}{}\ \overset{+4}{}\ \overset{+1}{}\ \overset{+3}{}\ \overset{+4}{}\ \overset{+1}{}$$
$$7 \quad 10 \quad 14 \quad 15 \quad 18 \quad 22 \quad 23 \quad \_\_$$

The overall pattern has now emerged. It is a repeat of +3+4+1. Therefore, it is obvious that the next number in the series, the final answer, is obtained by adding 3 to 23 to get 26.

What students have encountered here is a pattern composed of three different numbers, all of which are added in rotation to the numbers that occur in the series.

This new pattern is more complicated than the patterns in the first three examples, each of which had *one* number (4, 10, or 3), and *one* operation (addition, subtraction, or multiplication).

SERIES 5: 3 7 5 9 7 11 9 ___ ___

Series 4, though it had only one operation (addition), had three numbers.

Now, what would happen if students were given a number series with *two* operations and *two* numbers?

This is Series 5. Writing in the pattern, they get this:

$$\overset{+4}{}\overset{-2}{}\overset{+4}{}\overset{-2}{}\overset{+4}{}\overset{-2}{}$$
$$3 \quad 7 \quad 5 \quad 9 \quad 7 \quad 11 \quad 9 \; \_\_ \; \_\_$$

The answer becomes obvious at once. Adding 4 to 9, they get 13. And subtracting 2 from 13, they get 11.

In a number series, there can be any number of operations and any number of numbers to perform them on.

SERIES 6: 12 8 9 14 6 20 3 ___

But number series can get even *more* complicated. Take Series 6. Marking in our single pattern, we get this:

$$\overset{-4}{}\overset{+1}{}\overset{+5}{}\overset{-3}{}\overset{+14}{}\overset{-17}{}$$
$$12 \quad 8 \quad 9 \quad 14 \quad 6 \quad 20 \quad 3 \; \_\_$$

Here, there seems to be no pattern at all. And there is no single pattern. For a number series can also have *more* than one pattern in it. It can have two or more patterns.

But where are these patterns? Certainly not between the first and second or second and third numbers.

Then why not experiment? Why not try the first and third numbers, and then the third and fifth? And then the second and fourth numbers, and fourth and sixth?

If students try this, here is how the first every-other-number pattern will look:

$$\overset{-3}{}\quad\overset{-3}{}\quad\overset{-3}{}$$
$$12 \quad 8 \quad 9 \quad 14 \quad 6 \quad 20 \quad 3 \; \_\_$$

And here's how the second every-other-number pattern now looks:

$$\overset{-3}{}\quad\overset{-3}{}\quad\overset{-3}{}$$
$$12 \quad 8 \quad 9 \quad 14 \quad 6 \quad 20 \quad 3$$
$$\underset{+6}{}\quad\underset{+6}{}$$

Now the patterns have emerged, and the answer becomes clear. Add 6 to 20 and get the correct answer, 26.

SERIES 7: 2 4 8 3 9 27 4 ___ ___

And once they get used to the idea of two or more patterns in a single number series, even the most complicated problems of this type become a snap. In Series 7, for instance, they immediately spot the pattern as being this:

$$\underbrace{x2 \; x2}_{2 \; 4 \; 8} \quad \underbrace{x3 \; x3}_{3 \; 9 \; 27} \quad \underbrace{x4 \; x4}_{4 \_\_ \_\_}$$

They simply multiply 4 by 4 to get 16, and 16 by 4 to get 64, and they have the correct answer.

Again, as in all these number-series problems, the two-step technique works miracles in making the answer emerge. First, students discover the pattern. Then the pattern tells them the next number needed to complete the series.

Short-Answer Question Type 9: *Analogies*

An analogy question asks students to compare   **Definition**
one relation between two objects to another,
similar relation between two other objects. Its
usual form is "this is to that as something is to
something else."

HOURGLASS:CLOCK is most similar to: **What Analogies**
(1) acorn:oak   **Look Like**
(2) foundation:temple
(3) temple:church
(4) catapult:church
(5) catapult:cannon

Or, in a slightly different form:

Knowledge is to judgment as possession
is to _____.
(1) law
(2) acquisition
(3) use
(4) ignorance
(5) dispossession

Again, like the number-series question, the analogy question is composed of two parts, one of which is stated and the other hidden.

How to Master Analogy Questions

Find and State the Relation

The first step in solving an analogy question is to find, and state, the relation between the two objects that are given.

Find the Same Relation in the Answer List

The second step is to choose the two objects in the answer list that have the same relation as the given objects.

First, students find the relation between the two given objects, and write it down just as they wrote down the hidden pattern in the number-series questions. Then they find the other pair of objects in the answer list that have exactly the same relation.

For example, what is the relation between HOURGLASS and CLOCK?

Hourglass: clock

An hourglass is a *primitive* clock. It was the *forerunner* of the clock. So this *primitive, forerunner* relation is what students are looking for. They write it down, and begin testing each of the pairs in the answer list against it.

Not quite the same. An oak grows from an acorn, but a clock replaces an hourglass. The oak was inherent in the acorn, but a clock is an entirely different mechanism from an hourglass. Mark it no and go on.

Acorn: oak

No resemblance in the relation. A temple is built on a foundation, but a clock is not built in any way on the same foundation as an hourglass. No.

Foundation: temple

No. Two different houses of worship. Both exist at the present time. No resemblance.

Temple: church

No comparison.

Catapult: church

This looks like it. A catapult is a *primitive* cannon, just as an hourglass was a *primitive* clock. A catapult was a *forerunner* of the cannon, just as the hourglass was a *forerunner* of the clock. This is the correct answer. Mark it down and go on to the next question.

Catapult: cannon

What is the relation between KNOWLEDGE and JUDGMENT? They put the same technique to work:

Knowledge is a *requirement* for good judgment. To be a good judge, one *must have* knowledge. This is the relation students are looking for. They write it down—a *requirement*—and begin testing the pairs in the answer list against it.

Possession is not a requirement for law. No resemblance.

Possession: law

Possession is not a requirement for acquisition. They are practically synonymous. No resemblance.

Possession: acquisition

Possession is a requirement for use. You must possess something to use it. This looks like the correct answer. Students check it off, but still go on to each of the other possibilities to make absolutely certain.

Possession: use

No resemblance at all.

Possession: ignorance

No resemblance. They mean exactly the opposite.

Possession: dispossession

Therefore it must be *possession:use*. The correct answer emerges, once the hidden relation is brought out into the open.

Short-Answer Question Type 10:
The Combination Question

Finally, of course, many of the questions students will encounter on examinations will be
combinations of one or two of the types described above.

Definition

These combination questions can always be
solved by the step-by-step method. They are
first broken down into the number of steps it
takes to solve them, and then each step is done
in its turn.

**How to Master
Combination
Questions**

For example, take this question from a typical grade-school geography quiz:

Select the third letter of the word which correctly
completes the following statement:

Chicago is located in the state of:
(1)-I (2)-A (3)-N (4)-L (5)-O

There are two parts to this question. First, to find the state in which
Chicago is located, which is *Illinois.* Then, to find the third letter of
the word, *Illinois,* which is L. Thus the correct answer is 4.

Though the question may have seemed hard or confusing when
students first encountered it, it becomes simple as soon as they
break it down step by step.

A Note on IQ Tests

Throughout their school career, students will be judged by not one,
but two separate systems of grading.

The first system, of course, will be results in the exams given.

The second system of grading will be results in the IQ tests
given from time to time.

There is nothing mysterious or Godlike or absolutely final
about an IQ test. It is just another kind of test. What it measures is
not really students' innate intelligence, but simply their ability to pass
this type of test.

Therefore, as in any other test, grades can be improved by planning and practice. And, since this is probably the most important single test they will ever take in their school career, let us right now examine each one of the types of questions encountered on it, and how students can improve their performance on them.

1. Synonyms

Select the word which means the same.

BABY: **EXAMPLE**
1. son
2. infant
3. sister
4. born

1. Think up your own synonym before you   **Technique**
   read the list.
2. Read the entire list, crossing out wrong
   possibilities, and matching your synonym
   to the answer on the list.

2. Antonyms

Select the word which means the opposite.

BACK: **EXAMPLE**
1. side
2. front
3. top

1. Think up a synonym before you read the   **Technique**
   list.
2. Think of the word that means exactly the
   opposite.
3. Read the entire answer list to find this
   word and cross out the others.

3. Classification

Verbal cross-outs. Cross out the word that does not belong with the others.

1. daisy   **EXAMPLE**
2. rose
3. cat
4. lily

1. Read the entire list to discover the overall   **Technique**
    classification.
2. Write down the name of the classification.
3. Go over every word, crossing out the one
    that does not belong.

Beware of the first word on the list. It may be   **Warning**
the wrong one. Therefore read the entire list
before deciding on the overall classification.

4. Logical Reasoning

Special type of multiple-choice. Select the
word which tells what the first word *always*
has.

BOOK: **EXAMPLE**
1. pictures
2. pages
3. cover
4. story

Key word here is *always.* Not *sometimes* or   **Warning**
may possibly. But *always—without fail.* Therefore, even though a book may sometimes have
pictures, or a cover, or a story, it only has, *without fail,* pages, or it could not be a book.

1. Ask immediately, before reading the list,   **Technique**
    "A book *could only* be a book, *without fail,*
    if it had _____."
2. Write down the answer.
3. Read the entire list, matching your own
    answer, and crossing out the other possi-
    bilities as they do not fit.

5. Number Sequence

Filling in the next number in a given series.

EXAMPLE

What number should come next?
2 4 6 8 10 12 ___

Technique

1. Find out *what happens* in the series—establish the pattern between each of the numbers in the series.
2. Use this pattern to show you the next number.

6. Analogies

Given two objects with a specific relation, find a similar relation in two other objects.

EXAMPLE

Gun is to shoot as knife is to:
1. fly
2. meat
3. hurt
4. cut
5. hit

Technique

Again, use two steps.
1. Define the relation between the two given objects, and write it down.
2. Find the same relation between one of the possible answers, eliminating each of the others as you read it.

7. Proverbs

A kind of analogy. Given a famous proverb, find another statement among those furnished which means the same or most nearly the same.

EXAMPLE

Do Not Hang All On One Nail.
1. Don't count your chickens until they're hatched.

2. Don't put all your eggs in one basket.
3. Don't use a nail, use a hanger.

1. After reading the given proverb, before **Technique** you read the answer list, try to rephrase it in more general terms (for instance, in this example, try: "Don't risk all on one chance").
2. Read each of the possibilities, to find the one that matches your own rephrasing.

These, then, are the seven most used types of questions given on IQ tests. To help your son or daughter get the top possible grades they are capable of getting on these tests, go over these types of questions with them again and again. Make up new examples. Be sure they can use the right technique on each of them as easily as they can write their own name.

✔ IN SUMMARY ....

Students will encounter these ten types of short-answer questions on tests:

1. True-false
2. Multiple-choice
3. Completion
4. Enumeration
5. Sequence
6. Matching
7. Cross out
8. Number series
9. Analogies
10. Combinations

Through applying the proper techniques, each of these questions can be made simple, and even help furnish all or part of its own answer.

By giving students practice and more practice in solving each of them, you will turn them into test-room champions.

To the Student: Do It Yourself

To score well on short-answer tests, you must:

- Read with precision.
- Make judgments between right and wrong choices.
- Reason through a problem, step by step.
- Become familiar with the ten types of short-answer questions. They are:

1. True-false
2. Multiple-choice
3. Completion
4. Enumeration
5. Sequence
6. Matching
7. Cross out
8. Number series
9. Analogies
10. Combinations

- For IQ tests, be familiar with the types of questions asked. They are:

1. *Synonyms.* Select the word which means the same.
2. *Antonyms.* Select the word which means the opposite.
3. *Classification.* Verbal cross-outs. Cross out the word that does not belong with the others.
4. *Logical Reasoning.* Special type of multiple-choice. Select the word which tells what the first word always has.
5. *Number Sequence.* Filling in the next number in a given series.
6. *Analogies.* Given two objects with a specific relation, find a similar relation in two other objects.
7. *Proverbs.* A kind of analogy. Given a proverb, find another statement among those furnished which means the same or most nearly the same.

CHAPTER 24

THE ESSAY TEST

• • •

How to Master the Essay Test

The second great category of test that students will have to deal with in the examination room is the essay test. Unlike work at home, the essay tests do not, of course, give students the opportunity to rely on the computer to help with spelling, grammar, neatness, etc. They are on their own.

The essay test requires students to write. It confronts them with a question, or a series of questions, demanding lengthy, organized answers that may take up a full written page or more.

It tests the ability to:

1. Organize ideas
2. Express them clearly and logically

Therefore, on the essay test, your child is graded on two accomplishments:

1. What is said
2. How it is said

Let's see how we can help students get better grades in both these areas.

286

The Best Basic Strategy

We will, of course, assume that your child has prepared for the test in the manner outlined in this book. In other words, that he or she has absorbed and organized the material, arranged it in notes, reviewed the notes to eliminate any misunderstandings, and, above all, quizzed him or herself on the information in those notes by creating and answering a series of essay-type questions.

Because of this preparation, then, when your child enters the exam room, he or she is ready, not only with thoroughly organized material, but with some of the very questions that may be asked on the test.

With this bedrock background, your child follows this procedure:

1. He or she first reads the complete list of questions. In some essay exams, only one or two or three questions may make up the entire test. In others, there may be as many as ten questions, each demanding only a paragraph or two.

   Read the Complete List of Questions

   In any case, your child carefully reads them all, asking these two primary questions:

   Do I have to answer all the questions that are asked on this test, or does the test give me a choice?
   Either way, how many questions will I have to answer in the time I have allotted for this test?

2. Let us say, for example, that there are five essay questions that must be answered on the test. Once this face has been determined, your child now proceeds to *ration his or her time.* This is done in the following way:

   Ration Your Time

   The total amount of time allotted for the test must be determined—let us say two hours, or 120 minutes. Your child first sets aside twenty minutes at the end of this two hours to review what he or she has written and to correct any errors that may have been overlooked the first time.

This leaves 100 minutes of writing, in which five questions will have to be answered. Therefore, twenty minutes are allotted to each question.

Your child now has an overall time schedule set up, and can turn to the individual questions.

3. If the test does not demand that the questions be done in a specific order, he or she can arrange them in order and should do the easiest question first. The second-easiest second, and so on.

Answer the Easiest Question First

4. Now, each individual question gets its own time schedule. Each of the answers has two steps:

Outline Your Answer Before Starting to Write

- First it is outlined.
- Then it is written.

The outline is easily as important as the final written answer. It is in this outline that the idea backbone of the answer is built. The thoughts are organized that will later be put into sentences.

Therefore, for each answer, about one-fifth of the time should be taken to outline the answer, and the rest of the time used to write it out on the basis of that outline.

For example, four minutes to outline the answer and sixteen minutes of *guided* writing will result in a far better grade than twenty minutes

EXAMPLE

of blind writing. And the organization of the thoughts will shine right through.

And, above all, this way your child won't end up writing hurriedly, just getting to the point when the allotted time is almost over.

The Nineteen Key Essay-Question Words, and How to Answer Each of Them Correctly

Now, let's take a look at some of the essay questions that your child will be required to answer, and what must be done to get each of them precisely right.

The directions for most essay questions are built around nineteen key words. Your child must be familiar with what these words mean, and what the teacher expects your child's answer to look like.

Here are the nineteen key words teachers use in the directions for answering most essay questions:

1. Evaluate	8. Outline	15. Illustrate
2. Summarize	9. List	16. Interpret
3. Compare	10. Define	17. Justify
4. Explain	11. State	18. Prove
5. Criticize	12. Review	19. Contrast
6. Name	13. Describe	
7. Discuss	14. Enumerate	

Let's look at what each one of these key terms means, and what your child's teacher is looking for.

1. Evaluate

Evaluate the concept of "overlearning" as a sound study procedure. **Sample Question**

An evaluation is an appraisal, a weighing of pros and cons. Therefore, the answer should cite the advantages and disadvantages of the subject being discussed, and end with an opinion on its worth. **How to Answer It Correctly**

2. Summarize

Sample Question

Summarize the main economic causes of World War I.

How to Answer It Correctly

A summary is a condensed outline of main points. Therefore, *only the main points* should be given in a concise, outline form, omitting minor detail. Here, the bare outline will often do for the answer, if your child is in a hurry.

3. Compare

Sample Question

Compare standardized and teacher-made tests in respect to use in the classroom.

How to Answer It Correctly

A comparison is an examination of character or qualities, for the purpose of discovering resemblances or differences. Therefore, your child should first list the qualities of each of the two subjects to be compared, and then show how they resemble each other or how they differ. Your child is not required to evaluate them, or end up with an opinion on their comparative worth.

4. Explain

Sample Question

Explain the concept of a chain reaction.

How to Answer It Correctly

To explain is to make plain. Therefore, your child should show exactly how the subject works, in logical, step-by-step order. This happens, which causes this to happen, which causes this to happen.

5. Criticize

Sample Question

Criticize the statement, "One should study at least two hours for every hour spent in class."

How to Answer It Correctly

A criticism is an examination of a subject and then a judgment. Therefore, your child should first examine the evidence for and against the statement, and then give his or her opinion on its merits.

6. Name

Name three factors that are basic to school success. **Sample Question**

This is the easiest and shortest of all essay questions. Your child simply names the subjects asked for, without further detail. **How to Answer It Correctly**

7. Discuss

Discuss the role of the liver in digestion. **Sample Question**

To discuss something is to examine it from all angles. Therefore, your child should give the complete story of the subject asked for, from its beginning to its end. **How to Answer It Correctly**

8. Outline

Outline the principal steps in preparing an assignment. **Sample Question**

Your child has been outlining all year long. Therefore, he or she simply uses the primary outline as the final answer to this question. **How to Answer It Correctly**

9. List

List five suggestions that are applicable to preparing for examinations. **Sample Question**

A listing is simply a naming. Therefore, your child numbers the subjects asked for, and names them one after the other without further elaboration. **How to Answer It Correctly**

10. Define

Define the term "expletive." **Sample Question**

A definition is an explanation of the meaning of a word. Therefore, your child starts his or **How to Answer It Correctly** her definition with "An expletive is . . . ," and explains its meaning in the remainder of the sentence. Few words will require more than one sentence.

11. State

State three reasons why Mainland China was allowed into the United Nations.

Sample Question

To state is the same as to name. Therefore, your child uses the same procedure as that discussed for the key word "name."

How to Answer It Correctly

12. Review

Review the principal causes of the Stock Market crash of 1929.

Sample Question

Same as "discuss." Use same procedure.

How to Answer It Correctly

13. Describe

Describe the circulatory system in the human body.

Sample Question

A description is simply a narration without searching for causes. Therefore, your child simply follows through the process asked for, step by step, without giving any reasons for its cause or order.

How to Answer It Correctly

14. Enumerate

Enumerate the results of the falling of the Berlin Wall.

Sample Question

To enumerate is to list or name. Therefore, your child uses the technique described at those key words.

How to Answer It Correctly

15. Illustrate

Give three illustrations of President Clinton's foreign policy during his term in office.

Sample Question

To illustrate is to give examples. Therefore, your child names the number of examples required, describing them sufficiently to identify them, but neither evaluating them nor giving causes for their existence.

How to Answer It Correctly

16. Interpret

Interpret the Supreme Court ruling on integration in the University of Mississippi Case.

Sample Question

An interpretation is an explanation, usually in reference to a specific instance or viewpoint. Therefore, your child explains the consequence of the subject (in this case, the Supreme Court ruling) in the instance asked for (in this case, the University of Mississippi dispute.)

How to Answer It Correctly

17. Justify

Justify the statement, "All behavior is ultimately caused by circumstances outside the individual."

Sample Question

A justification is a marshaling of reasons favoring a statement. Therefore, your child lists each of the facts that support the statement given, and shows how they combine to give grounds for believing it.

How to Answer It Correctly

18. Prove

What is the proof of the second law of thermodynamics?

Sample Question

Proof is double evidence—first that a statement is correct, and second that an opposite statement must be false. Therefore, your child lists the facts that serve as evidence for the given statement, and then supplements them with further facts that disprove any contradictory statements.

How to Answer It Correctly

19. Contrast

Contrast standardized and teacher-made tests in respect to use in the classroom. **Sample Question**

To contrast two objects is to bring out their differences. Therefore, your child should list the differences between the two objects mentioned in the question, difference by difference. He or she is not required to list their similarities or evaluate them. **How to Answer It Correctly**

Tips on Raising Your Child's Answers Above the Ordinary Level

Once a student has identified the exact way he or she will respond to each key word, and outlined an answer to each question, he or she then proceeds to write out the answers on the test paper. To improve grades, your child follows these simple rules:

5. Handwriting tricks should not be used. Your child should write clearly and neatly, with large indentations at the beginning of each paragraph. **Write Clearly and Neatly**

6. For every answer, your child should adopt a position and then stick to it. This position should be declared in the first sentence of each answer, in this way: **Summarize the Position in the First Sentence**

   Teacher-made tests are far superior to standardized tests for the following reasons: . . .

7. Where possible, each answer should be documented with detailed supporting evidence. Once your child has memorized the backbone facts, then many concrete details will be carried along in his or her memory with them. These details should be used **State Specific Facts Supporting the Position**

everywhere they occur, to be as specific as possible.

For example, your child should not say:

Man needs a certain minimum daily food intake.

If possible, he or she should be more specific:

A man weighing 165 pounds needs as many as 4,500 calories per day.

This adds color and believability to the main points. But make sure your child gets the main points down first, and then fills in the details.

8. Certain easy-to-use devices add great excitement and believability to the answers—make the examination paper stand out head and shoulders above the common crowd. Have your child use as many of the following devices as possible: **Enhance the Answer with Visual Aids**
   - Diagrams
   - Graphs
   - Outlines
   - Underlined sections
   - Technical terms
   - Illustrations and examples

9. Cross references save time, squeeze more information into each question, impress readers. They are a simple method of quoting part of one question to help document another. **Use Cross References**

For example, your child might use a cross reference in this way:

Teacher-made tests are also superior to the standardized version for the reasons stated in answers 2(b) and 3(c) given above.

10. There is no reason to argue with the position taken by the teacher in the exam statements. Your child should take the teacher's position as his or her own and develop it *as given*.

   Take the Teacher's Position as Given

11. And your child should never, never use slang. Good English and good logic should be used throughout.

   Never Use Slang

What a Student Does in the Last Twenty Minutes

12. The last twenty minutes are saved as a safety factor. When reaching them, your child should stop writing, no matter how far along into the test.

   Save Twenty Minutes for Review

13. If all the answers are finished, he or she now carefully reads them, correcting spelling and punctuation, checking them against the outline to make sure every main point is included.

   Check the Answers

   If your child wishes to add a final idea, it should be done at the bottom of the question, beginning it with a statement such as:

   One further point that increases the superiority of teacher-made tests even further . . .

14. If, however, your child has not finished that "one last question," he or she uses half this twenty minutes to answer it in this way:

   Use an Outline If Time Runs Out

   A formal outline of the answer is made. This formal outline touches on all aspects of the answer, using clear, concise sentences for each main point. If the outline is valid and clear enough, and if the other answers show a mature writing style, your child may receive full credit for this outline answer as well.

15. Above all, every second of time allowed by the test should be used to make sure the answers are the absolute best he or she can make them. **Make Every Second Count**

In all these answers, your child should give exactly what is called for. Neither more nor less than is expected. Clear, concise, to the point. And then go on to the next question.

IN SUMMARY

Essay tests are graded on two separate accomplishments:

1. The organization of ideas.
2. Their clear and logical expression.

Therefore, to get top grades on an essay test, a plan of attack is essential.

During the test, about one-sixth of your child's time should be devoted to outlining the answers, two-thirds of the time to writing out the essays, and the remaining one-sixth of the time to checking that writing to correct any omissions or errors.

Each answer should give exactly what is called for in the question. Therefore, your child should know what each essay-test key word demands, and be immediately ready to satisfy it.

To the Student: Do It Yourself

- Organize your ideas.
- Express them clearly and logically on paper.

SPECIFICALLY

- Read the complete list of questions asked on the test.
- If permitted, arrange the order of the questions so you can answer the easiest first.
- Find the key word in each question. To review, these words are:

Evaluate	*Summarize*	*Compare*	*Explain*
Criticize	*Name*	*Discuss*	*Outline*
List	*Define*	*State*	*Review*
Describe	*Enumerate*	*Illustrate*	*Interpret*
Justify	*Prove*	*Contrast*	

- Ration the amount of time you spend on each question.
- Outline your answers, using one-sixth of the allotted time.
- Write your answers clearly, using two-thirds of the time.
- For every answer, adopt a position and stick to it.
- Document each answer with detailed supportive evidence.
- Add credibility to your answers, when possible, with:

Diagrams / Graphs / Outlines / Technical Terms
Underlined Sections / Illustrations / Examples

- Cross-reference your answers when possible.
- Take the teacher's position when possible.
- Never use slang.
- Use the last one-sixth (ten minutes in a one-hour exam) of the time to:
  1. Review your answer.
  2. Check spelling, punctuation.
  3. See that you have included everything from your outline.
  4. Add additional points.
  5. Finish an unfinished question by outlining your answer.

MAKING TESTS ANSWER THEMSELVES

• • •

The Test Itself Can Help a Student Pass

Now that your child is familiar with the types of questions that he or she will encounter in tests and has been drilled in the proper way to answer each of them, let us now bring all these test-taking skills together, and see how to use them to pull out a top grade in an actual examination.

We have already done this for an essay-type test. Now we will set up the same strategy—the same professional time schedule— for the hundreds of short-answer tests that will be taken during your child's lifetime.

Here goes. Your son or daughter is on the way to another test-taking triumph.

The First Five Minutes

A student's first goal, when entering the room, is always to overcome whatever nervousness he or she may have brought along. Any student wants to take this test calmly and coolly, in complete charge of all the information he or she has acquired.

For this reason, the first five minutes are crucial. It is during these five minutes that the student either settles down to productive work and makes the test work for him or her, or gives way to panic and mind-blocking. In order to avoid this, the following simple procedure should be adhered to:

1. The pencil should stay on the desk and not be picked up for five minutes.   **Don't Panic**

2. These five minutes are used to *pre-read* the exam. To become familiar with the entire exam before doing any part of it. To read all directions *twice*. To look especially for the following points: **Pre-Read the Exam**

   A. What are the exact instructions? Are the answers to be given in any special way? Is there a choice of questions, or does every question have to be answered?   **Answer These Pre-Reading Questions First**

   B. Are there any questions that were anticipated? If so, they will give a big boost to your child's confidence.

   C. How long is the exam? Will there be a time problem? If so, starting on the easiest or most familiar questions, skipping those he or she doesn't know and coming back to them later if there is time, is the most efficient use of the time allotted.

   D. What parts of the exam give the most credit? These will be done first, if the answers are known.

   E. Are there any questions that are closely related? If so, your child will make sure not to give the same answer on both.

F. Do any questions give the answer, or suggest the answer, to another question? This happens far too often to be overlooked, and can add as much as 10 percent to 15 percent to the grade.

3. All these pre-reading questions must be answered *before* picking up a pen to actually begin writing the exam. **Pre-Reading for Calm and Confidence**

At this point, your child will be calm, confident, and deliberate, without a trace of the emotional overexcitement that could spell disaster.

Writing the Exam: How to Avoid Careless Errors

In the actual writing of the exam, of course, the second great danger occurs. This is plain ordinary carelessness, the malady that causes more test failures than anything else but sheer neglect of study.

Here are some of the most frequent mistakes caused by nothing else but sheer carelessness:

The student fails to read the question *correctly,* missing key words or missing their meaning. **Read Carefully**

The student reads only part of a question, and then starts to answer without reading the rest of the question. But that last part of the question may change its meaning entirely. **Read the Whole Question**

The student makes a list when asked to explain. Or gives incidents and events, rather than the causes for them. Or compares when asked to contrast. Or writes long, detailed lists of reasons, when asked to give the main reason only. **Make a List of Reasons**

Such patterns of carelessness are constant. When your son or daughter develops one of them, he or she will repeat it over and over again, unless you help stamp it out.

Therefore, as we have said before, study your child's *particular pattern of carelessness* BEFORE he or she gets in the test room. And then correct it, day by day, till it is completely eradicated, and your child will never slip back into it, even under the most extreme pressure.

Writing the Exam: Making Sure That Each Answer Is Correct

4. Now your child picks up a pencil and begins to take the test. The first step is to go back to the questions he or she is sure of, and answer them first. **Answer Known Questions First**

5. Your child uses these correct answers, plus the information given in the other test questions, plus the techniques of making questions solve themselves that we have described in Chapter 22, to work through the remaining questions that he or she is not completely sure of. **Use These Questions to Solve Remaining Questions**

6. These are solved one question at a time. The student reads each twice to make sure it is understood. He or she concentrates on it exclusively, without glancing at the remaining questions until it is finished, then goes on to the next one. **Read Each Question Twice**

7. Your child must always strive for neatness, good order, and correct spelling, grammar, and punctuation where required. **Strive for Neatness**

8. He or she tries to allot five or ten minutes after finishing the test to review it. This time is used to check back over the test to make sure there are no careless mistakes or omissions. He or she does not, however, **Allow Five to Ten Minutes for Review**

"second-guess" the answers, but relies instead on the first intuitive answer unless new information has been uncovered further along in the test that makes him or her sure there is a better answer.

9. If there are answers still unfinished, or questions your child does not know, he or she follows this rule:

    If the test does not penalize for guessing or wrong answers, and if an unanswered question will be graded wrong anyway, then the best possible guess should be made.

    If, however, the test penalizes for guessing in any way, your child simply leaves these questions blank.

    Guessing or Not Depends on Whether There Is a Penalty for Wrong Answers

10. Again, your child uses every second of the time given. He or she checks and rechecks to make sure there are no correctable mistakes, no omissions, and that the absolute top grade he or she is capable of has been squeezed out.

    Then the paper is handed in and forgotten. Because your child knows that the job has been done—and done well—and he or she can confidently await the reward.

    Use Every Second

And be sure you echo this reward of praise when the final grades are in.

Praise a Job Well Done

✔ IN SUMMARY ....

In taking any test, your child must first concentrate on eliminating:

1. Overexcitement and emotional block
2. Careless mistakes

Once this has been done, he or she then concentrates on making one part of the test help solve the other, as we have shown you in these chapters.

These three basic techniques add up to top grades on any test that can be thrown at a student. Exercised properly, they give your child an enormous advantage over any other student in that test room.

To the Student: Do It Yourself

- Take each test calmly and coolly. First put down your pencil for five minutes and pre-read the exam. Read all directions twice.
- Ask yourself what are the exact instructions? Are the answers to be given in any special way? Is there a choice of questions or do you have to answer them all?
- Determine how long the exam is. Can you finish it all? Which parts give the most credit? (Start with these, if you know the answers.)
- Figure out if any questions give you answers or hints of answers to any other questions.
- Avoid carelessness. Often that means failing to read the question correctly, or reading only part of the question.
- Answer the questions you are sure of first.
- Work on the others later, using any information from other questions in answering them.
- Strive for neatness, good order, correct spelling, good grammar and punctuation.
- Try to leave five or ten minutes at the end to check your test over.
- Fill in any omitted questions or unfinished questions that you know.
- Guess *only* if you are not penalized for doing so.

CHAPTER

ATTENTION DEFICIT DISORDER

• • •

What to Do If Your Child Has It

To get top grades in school, your child must have a basic ability to pay attention while learning. If he or she is having problems, your child's teacher may tell you that your child should be tested for Attention Deficit Disorder (ADD). Or you may already have an evaluation which states that your child has this condition.

What Is ADD?

A child diagnosed with ADD shows one or more of the following behaviors—but not all the time.

1. Squirms and fidgets during studying ses-   **ADD**
   sions.   **Characteristics**
2. Needs reminding every few minutes to
   keep working.
3. Disturbs class.
4. Daydreams.
5. Loses concentration.

6. Speak out of turn.
7. Get distracted easily.
8. Follow directions poorly.
9. Act impulsively.
10. Become frustrated often.

A diagnosis is difficult because a child's behavior can very often depend on many factors, including time, place, and situation. At times, even evaluators have different opinions, one saying a child has ADD, and another saying the same child's behavior is normal for his or her age. Some educators feel that the time given to deciding if a child has ADD would be better spent on finding ways to overcome the attention problems.

While experts do not agree on the causes of ADD, they recognize that it is a biochemical condition. However, labeling your child is not always necessary, because the right study plan will find the way to break through any blocks to your child's potential.

Many successful people have been diagnosed as having ADD. Learning coping techniques allows them to thrive in whatever they choose to do.

Some children who have a diagnosis of ADD also have learning differences or disorders. Dyslexia, a learning disorder affecting reading ability, occurs in about 25 percent of those who have ADD. Proper learning skills will make up for the difficulties in reading, mathematics, and writing.

You may or may not have a diagnosis and recommendations by educational and medical professionals. But this is not always necessary. The techniques already given in this book, if followed carefully, will help the typical problems of children with ADD.

Be assured. The study plan in this book has sound learning principles that work for all children, even those who are hard to reach because of emotional or learning disorders.

What helps your child with ADD most is one-on-one help from a teacher, a tutor, or you yourself. Sitting each night with your child, and following the daily schedule, will get him or her to focus on tasks better than ever before.

And your child will carry these habits into the classroom each day. He or she will have the chance to work with a clear mind.

You also want to follow some extra tips, to help your ADD child even more. These strategies work along with the other procedures given in this book.

Extra Tips for Helping the Child with ADD

Here are some extra ways to keep your ADD child free of distractions. All of them are easy to *add* to his or her study plan.

They are:

1. Pay extra attention to your child's workplace, making sure all supplies—paper, pens, pencils, sharpeners, erasers, rulers—always have a special place, such as a drawer or case.

   Pay Attention to Your Child's Workplace

2. Keep all work in a box. Your child must keep all notebooks and books in this box when not using them. That way, he or she knows where materials are at all times. And see-through ziplock bags or nylon mesh bags to separate pencils are very helpful.

   Keep All Work in One Box

3. Create file folders to organize returned homework assignments, tests, and papers. Establish separate files for each subject. Within each subject file, there can be separate folders for tests returned, projects to be completed, etc. This will enable your child to easily access this information during test periods and exam times.

   Create a File for Each Subject

4. Keep all supplies, such as pens, pencils, markers, and notebook paper in labeled plastic bags or boxes for easy access.

   Keep Supplies Labeled

5. Time the work sessions to increase his or her ability to concentrate. Start with the shortest period, say two to five minutes, and then work up to thirty minutes. Take one-minute breaks in between timing.

   Time the Work Sessions

6. Focus your child quickly with nonverbal cues, like raising your hand or pointing to an assignment when you see that he or she has lost concentration.

   Help Focus with Nonverbal Clues

7. Make daily detailed "to do" lists to organize nonschool tasks like mailing letters, walking the dog, and calling friends or relatives. Always keep them in the same place.

   Make "To Do" Lists

8. Use calming music during rest periods. Some ADD children actually benefit from listening to music while studying because the music helps block out distractions for them. Try out various types, such as classical or "new age," for their effect on your child.

   Use Music to Calm Your Child

9. Breathing exercises before starting to work can help relax and focus your child. Have him or her breathe in while letting the stomach expand and breathe out while letting the stomach contract. Do this five times.

   Breathing Exercises Will Focus the Mind

Most of All

10. Believe in your child's ability to succeed.

    Believe in Your Child's Innate Ability

With your ADD child, you are heading for one goal: building routine and making that routine automatic. Everything—from setting out pencils and paper, to turning on the light, from sitting down at the same place at the same time each day, to taking breaks after certain tasks are done—needs to become second nature. Just as much second nature as the way your child brushes his or her teeth each morning and night.

And, if these extra steps are followed, you will reap the reward of seeing how he or she can gain control over that most important behavior—that of paying attention to the tasks at hand.

 IN SUMMARY ....

If your child has an attention disorder, you can help to overcome his or her problems.

- Follow the step-by-step plan in this book for helping your child to double his or her grades in school.
- Add extra strategies to help your child overcome attention difficulties.
- Establish a routine for success that becomes automatic.

To the Student: Do It Yourself

- Do not worry if you have been told you have ADD.
- You can overcome problems you have with paying attention by working through the step-by-step method in this book with your parent or a friend.
- Make sure you have a set routine way of studying each day.
- Keep your materials in order. Mark them with a label in large letters so everything is instantly identifiable. A magic marker helps. Set up a file clearly marked for every subject. A desk drawer or a file on top of the table will do.
- Also, by talking about it with the people you work with, you can have them help you.

EPILOGUE

. . .

How to Make Your Child into
a Classroom Champion

There it is. You now have the techniques you need to double your child's grades in school.

They are simple, fast, and enormously effective. Used properly, they can get your child into the Rapid-Advancement Class that might otherwise reject him or her, can get your child the A's and B's that he or she might otherwise have just barely missed, can get your child into the college of his or her choice and the dream job that might otherwise have passed by.

But they can't do a single one of these things without your active support!

Reading these techniques—even learning them—is just not enough. Teaching them to your child is not enough. Even demanding that your child memorize them is not enough.

They are no good to you—or your child—until they become SECOND NATURE. Until they are built into the nervous system as reaction patterns or habits. Until they can be done automatically— perfectly—without thinking. As easily and quickly and naturally as your child writes his or her name.

And this means PRACTICE!
PRACTICE!
PRACTICE!

Champions in any field, whether it be art, or sports, or business, or study, are made by two great tools:

1. Knowledge or technique.
2. Practice to perfect that technique.

The first element, knowledge, can be bought. It can be bought in the form of a book, or a lecture, or even in the form of hard experience.

But the second element, practice, can only be earned. It is a function of character. It is a result of that inner drive, persistence, endurance, patience, will to win, refusal to quit, that makes the champion.

In life, it is not intelligence that makes the great difference. We have all seen too many brilliant minds left panting behind—shattered and defeated—doomed to lives of nameless mediocrity.

In life, ultimately, *it is drive that counts!* The tortoise still wins; the hare is left sleeping in obscurity!

"A winner never quits; a quitter never wins!"

"Practice makes perfect."

This is old wisdom. True wisdom. Wisdom that works today in the science laboratory as much as it did in the groves of Socratic Greece.

Teach it to your child. Build into your child, not only the techniques that produce success, but the drive that will settle for nothing less than success, and you will give him or her the greatest gift next to love that it will ever be in your power to hand on.

Good luck. And good teaching.

INDEX

Page numbers in *boldface italic* are illustrations.